GRE® Exam
Vocabulary Prep

The Staff of Kaplan Test Prep and Admissions

PUBLISHING

New York

This publication is designed to provide accurate and authoritative information in regard to the subject matter covered. It is sold with the understanding that the publisher is not engaged in rendering legal, accounting, or other professional service. If legal advice or other expert assistance is required, the services of a competent professional should be sought.

© 2008 Kaplan, Inc.

Published by Kaplan Publishing, a division of Kaplan, Inc.
1 Liberty Plaza, 24th Floor
New York, NY 10006

Printed in the United States of America

August 2008
10 9 8 7 6 5 4 3 2 1

ISBN-13: 978-1-4195-5002-7

Kaplan Publishing books are available at special quantity discounts to use for sales promotions, employee premiums, or educational purposes. Please email our Special Sales Department to order or for more information at kaplanpublishing@kaplan.com, or write to Kaplan Publishing, 1 Liberty Plaza, 24th Floor, New York, NY 10006.

HOW TO USE THIS BOOK

Kaplan's *GRE* Exam Vocabulary Prep* is perfectly designed to help you learn nearly 500 of the hardest, most essential GRE vocabulary words in a quick, easy, and fun way.

On the front of each page, you'll find three GRE vocabulary words along with its part of speech and pronunciation. On the back, you'll find the definitions and synonyms, as well as a sample sentence with the vocabulary word in action.

Feel free to skip over words once you've mastered them: Just cut off or fold back the corners of the page that correspond to the word you know, so you can flip right by it on your next pass through the book.

Good luck!

Abeyance
noun
(uh <u>bay</u> uhns)

. . . .

Abstain
verb
(uhb <u>stayn</u>)

. . . .

Abyss
noun
(uh <u>bihs</u>)

temporary suppression or suspension

> *The baseball game was held in **abeyance** while it continued to rain.*

Synonyms: deferral; delay; dormancy; postponement; remission

. . . .

to choose not to do something

> *Before the medical procedure, you must **abstain** from eating.*

Synonyms: forbear; refrain; withhold

. . . .

an extremely deep hole

> *The submarine dove into the **abyss** to chart the previously unseen depths.*

Synonyms: chasm; void

Acme
noun
(<u>aak</u> mee)

· ·

Adulterate
verb
(uh <u>duhl</u> tuhr ayt)

· ·

Advocate
verb
(<u>aad</u> vuh kayt)

highest point; summit; the highest level or degree attainable

> *Just when he reached the **acme** of his power, the dictator was overthrown.*

Synonyms: apex; peak; summit

• •

to make impure

> *The restaurateur made his ketchup last longer by **adulterating** it with water.*

Synonyms: debase; doctor; load

• •

to speak in favor of

> *The vegetarian **advocated** a diet containing no meat.*

Synonyms: back; champion; support

Aerie
noun
(<u>ayr</u> ee) (<u>eer</u> ee)

• •

Aesthetic
adj
(ehs <u>theh</u> tihk)

• •

Affected
adj
(uh <u>fehk</u> tihd)

a nest built high in the air; an elevated, often secluded, dwelling

*Perched high among the trees, the eagle's **aerie** was filled with eggs.*

Synonyms: perch; stronghold

• •

concerning the appreciation of beauty

*The **Aesthetic** Movement regarded the pursuit of beauty to be the only true purpose of art.*

Synonyms: artistic; tasteful

• •

phony; artificial

*The **affected** hairdresser spouted French phrases, though she had never been to France.*

Synonyms: insincere; pretentious; put-on

Alleviate
verb
(uh <u>lee</u> vee ayt)

. . . .

Amalgamate
verb
(uh <u>maal</u> guh mayt)

. . . .

Ambiguous
adj
(aam <u>bihg</u> yoo uhs)

to make more bearable

> *Taking aspirin helps to **alleviate** a headache.*

Synonyms: allay; assuage; comfort; ease; lessen; lighten; mitigate; palliate; relieve

. . . .

to combine; to mix together

> *Giant Industries **amalgamated** with Mega Products to form Giant-Mega Products Incorporated.*

Synonyms: admix; blend; coalesce; combine; commingle; commix; compound; fuse; intermingle; intermix; merge; mingle; mix; unite

. . . .

doubtful; uncertain; can be interpreted several ways

> *The directions he gave were so **ambiguous** that we disagreed on which way to turn.*

Synonyms: cloudy; doubtful; dubious; equivocal; indeterminate; nebulous; obscure; unclear; vague

Amulet
noun
(<u>aam</u> yoo liht)

· ·

Analogous
adj
(uh <u>naal</u> uh guhs)

· ·

Antagonize
verb
(aan <u>taa</u> guh niez)

ornament worn as a charm against evil spirits

> *Though she claimed it was not because of superstition, Vivian always wore an **amulet** around her neck.*

Synonyms: fetish; talisman

• •

similar or alike in some way; equivalent to

> *His mother argued that not going to college was **analogous** to throwing his life away.*

Synonyms: alike; comparable; corresponding; equivalent; homogeneous; parallel; similar

• •

to annoy or provoke to anger

> *The child discovered that he could **antagonize** the cat by pulling its tail.*

Synonyms: clash; conflict; incite; irritate; oppose; pester; provoke; vex

Apathy
noun
(<u>aa</u> pah thee)

· ·

Arbitrary
adj
(<u>ah r</u> bih trayr ee)

· ·

Arbitrate
verb
(<u>ahr</u> bih trayt)

lack of interest or emotion

> *The **apathy** of voters is so great that less than half the people who are eligible to vote actually bother to do so.*

Synonyms: coolness; disinterest; disregard; impassivity; indifference; insensibility; lassitude; lethargy; listlessness; phlegm; stolidity; unconcern; unresponsiveness

• •

determined by chance or impulse

> *When you lack the information to judge what to do next, you will be forced to make an **arbitrary** decision.*

Synonyms: changeable; erratic; indiscriminate; random; wayward

• •

to judge a dispute between two opposing parties

> *Since the couple could not come to an agreement, a judge was forced to **arbitrate** their divorce proceedings.*

Synonyms: adjudge; adjudicate; determine; intermediate; intervene; judge; moderate; referee; rule

Archaic
adj
(ahr <u>kay</u> ihk)

. . . .

Articulate
adj
(ahr <u>tih</u> kyuh luht)

. . . .

Assail
verb
(uh <u>sayl</u>)

ancient; old-fashioned

*Her **archaic** Commodore computer could not run the latest software.*

Synonyms: ancient; antediluvian; antique; archaic; bygone; dated; dowdy; fusty; obsolete; old-fashioned; outdated; outmoded; passé; prehistoric; stale; superannuated; superseded; vintage

• •

able to speak clearly and expressively

*She is extremely **articulate** when it comes to expressing her pro-labor views; as a result, unions are among her strongest supporters.*

Synonyms: eloquent; expressive; fluent; lucid; silver-tongued; smooth-spoken

• •

to attack; assault

*The foreign army will try to **assail** our bases, but they will not be successful in their attack.*

Synonyms: beset; strike; storm

Audacious
adj
(aw <u>day</u> shuhs)

....

Austere
adj
(aw <u>steer</u>)

....

Axiom
noun
(<u>aak</u> see uhm)

fearless; daring

> The **audacious** peasant dared to insult the king's mother.

Synonyms: adventuresome; aggressive; assertive; bold; brave; courageous; daring; dauntless; doughty; fearless; gallant; game; heroic; intrepid; mettlesome; plucky; stout; stouthearted; unafraid; undaunted; valiant; valorous; venturesome; venturous

• •

severe or stern in appearance; undecorated

> The lack of decoration makes Zen temples seem **austere** to the untrained eye.

Synonyms: bleak; dour; grim; hard; harsh; severe

• •

premise; postulate; self-evident truth

> Halle lived her life based on the **axioms** her grandmother had passed on to her.

Synonyms: adage; apothegm; aphorism; maxim; rule

Banal
adj
(buh <u>naal</u>) (<u>bay</u> nuhl) (buh <u>nahl</u>)

. . . .

Belfry
noun
(<u>behl</u> free)

. . . .

Bombastic
adj
(bahm <u>baast</u> ihk)

predictable; clichéd; boring

*His conversation consisted of **banal** phrases like 'Have a nice day' or 'Another day, another dollar.'*

Synonyms: bland; bromidic; clichéd; commonplace; fatuous; hackneyed; innocuous; insipid; jejune; musty; platitudinous; prosaic; quotidian; shopworn; stale; stereotypic; threadbare; timeworn; tired; trite; vapid; worn-out

• •

bell tower; room in which a bell is hung

*The town was shocked when a bag of money was found stashed in the old **belfry** of the church.*

Synonyms: spire; steeple

• •

pompous in speech and manner

*Mussolini's speeches were mostly **bombastic**; his boasting and outrageous claims had no basis in fact.*

Synonyms: bloated; declamatory; fustian; grandiloquent; grandiose; high-flown; magniloquent; orotund; pretentious; rhetorical; self-important

Boor
noun
(bohr)

• •

Burnish
vorb
(<u>buhr</u> nihsh)

• •

Catalyst
noun
(<u>kaa</u> tuh lihst)

crude person; one lacking manners or taste

> *"That utter **boor** ruined my recital with his constant guffawing!" wailed the pianist.*

Synonyms: clod; lout; oaf; vulgarian; yahoo

• •

to polish

> *He **burnished** the silver coffee pot until it shone brightly.*

Synonyms: buff; luster; polish; scour

• •

something that brings about a change in something else

> *The imposition of harsh taxes was the **catalyst** that finally brought on the revolution.*

Synonyms: accelerator; goad; impetus; impulse; incentive; motivation; spur; stimulant

Chaos
noun
(<u>kay</u> ahs)

. . . .

Coalesce
verb
(koh uh <u>lehs</u>)

. . . .

Connoisseur
noun
(kah nuh <u>suhr</u>)

great disorder; confused situation

> *In most religious traditions, God created an ordered universe from **chaos**.*

Synonyms: clutter; confusion; disarrangement; disarray; disorder; disorderliness; disorganization; jumble; mess; muddle; scramble; snarl; topsy-turviness; turmoil

· ·

to grow together to form a single whole

> *The sun and planets eventually **coalesced** out of a vast cloud of gas and dust.*

Synonyms: amalgamate; blend; coalesce; condense; consolidate; fuse; unite

· ·

a person with expert knowledge or discriminating tastes

> *Dr. Crane was a **connoisseur** of fine food and wine, drinking and eating only the best.*

Synonyms: authority; epicure; expert; gastronome; gourmet

Convoluted
adj
(kahn vuh <u>loo</u> tehd)

· ·

Crescendo
noun
(kruh <u>shehn</u> doh)

· ·

Debutante
noun
(<u>dehb</u> yoo tahnt)

intricate and complicated

*Although many people bought the professor's book, few people could follow its **convoluted** ideas and theories.*

Synonyms: Byzantine; complex; elaborate; intricate; knotty; labyrinthine; perplexing; tangled

. . . .

steadily increasing in volume or force

*The **crescendo** of tension became unbearable as Evel Knievel prepared to jump his motorcycle over the school buses.*

Synonyms: acme, capstone, climax, crest, culmen, culmination, meridian, peak

. . . .

young woman making debut in high society

*The **debutante** spent hours dressing for her very first ball, hoping to catch the eye of an eligible bachelor.*

Synonyms: lady; maiden

Deface
verb
(dih <u>fays</u>)

. . . .

Deference
noun
(<u>deh</u> fuh ruhn(t)s) (<u>def</u> ruhn(t)s)

. . . .

Demagogue
noun
(<u>deh</u> muh gahg) (<u>deh</u> muh gawg)

to mar the appearance of; vandalize

> *After the wall was torn down, the students began to* ***deface*** *the statues of Communist leaders of the former Eastern bloc.*

Synonyms: disfigure; impair; spoil

. . . .

respect; courtesy

> *The respectful young law clerk treated the Supreme Court justice with the utmost* ***deference***.

Synonyms: courtesy; homage; honor; obeisance; respect; reverence; veneration

. . . .

a rabble-rouser, usually appealing to emotion or prejudice

> *He began his career as a* ***demagogue***, *giving fiery speeches at political rallies.*

Synonyms: agitator; inciter; instigator

Dilate
verb
(<u>die</u> layt) (die <u>layt</u>)

. . . .

Dilettante
noun
(<u>dih</u> luh tahnt)

. . . .

Dirge
noun
(duhrj)

to make larger; expand

*When you enter a darkened room, the pupils of your eyes **dilate** so as to let in more light.*

Synonyms: amplify; develop; elaborate; enlarge; expand; expatiate

• •

someone with an amateurish and superficial interest in a topic

*Jerry's friends were such **dilettantes** they seemed to have new jobs and hobbies every week.*

Synonyms: amateur; dabbler; superficial; tyro

• •

a funeral hymn or mournful speech

*Melville wrote the poem "A **Dirge** for James McPherson" for the funeral of a Union general who was killed in 1864.*

Synonyms: elegy; lament

Discern
verb
(dihs <u>uhrn</u>)

. . . .

Disparate
adj
(<u>dih</u> spuh ruht) (di <u>spar</u> uht)

. . . .

Dither
verb
(<u>dihth</u> uhr)

to perceive or recognize

> *It is easy to **discern** the difference between butter and butter-flavored topping.*

Synonyms: catch; descry; detect; differentiate; discriminate; distinguish; espy; glimpse; know; separate; spot; spy; tell

· ·

fundamentally different; entirely unlike

> *Although the twins are physically identical, their personalities are **disparate**.*

Synonyms: different; dissimilar; divergent; diverse; variant; various

· ·

to act confusedly or without clear purpose

> *Ellen **dithered** around her apartment, uncertain how to tackle the family crisis.*

Synonyms: falter; hesitate; vacillate; waffle; waver

Dogma
noun
(<u>dahg</u> muh) (<u>dawg</u> muh)

• •

Dogmatic
adj
(dahg <u>maat</u> ihk) (dawg <u>maat</u> ihk)

• •

Elegy
noun
(<u>eh</u> luh jee)

a firmly held opinion, especially a religious belief

> *Linus' central **dogma** was that children who believed in The Great Pumpkin would be rewarded.*

Synonyms: creed; doctrine; teaching; tenet

•••••••••••••••••••••••••••••••••

dictatorial in one's opinions

> *The dictator was **dogmatic**, claiming he, and only he, was right.*

Synonyms: authoritarian; bossy; dictatorial; doctrinaire; domineering; imperious; magisterial; masterful; overbearing; peremptory

•••••••••••••••••••••••••••••••••

a sorrowful poem or speech

> *Though Thomas Gray's **Elegy** is about death and loss, it urges its readers to endure this life, and to trust in spirituality.*

Synonyms: dirge; lament

Eloquent
adj
(<u>ehl</u> uh kwunt)

. . . .

Embellish
verb
(ehm <u>behl</u> ihsh)

. . . .

Enigma
noun
(ih <u>nig</u> muh)

persuasive and moving, especially in speech

*The Gettysburg Address is moving not only because of its lofty sentiments but because of its **eloquent** words.*

Synonyms: articulate; expressive; fluent; meaningful; significant; smooth-spoken

· ·

to add ornamental or fictitious details

*Britt **embellished** her résumé, hoping to make the lowly positions she had held seem more important.*

Synonyms: adorn; bedeck; elaborate; embroider; enhance; exaggerate

· ·

a puzzle; a mystery

*Speaking in riddles and dressed in old robes, the artist gained a reputation as something of an **enigma**.*

Synonyms: conundrum; perplexity

Erratic
adj
(ih <u>raat</u> ihk)

· ·

Esoteric
adj
(eh suh <u>tehr</u> ihk)

· ·

Ethos
noun
(<u>ee</u> thohs)

wandering and unpredictable

*The plot seemed predictable until it suddenly took a series of **erratic** turns that surprised the audience.*

Synonyms: capricious; inconstant; irresolute; whimsical

• •

known or understood only by a few

*Only a handful of experts are knowledgeable about the **esoteric** world of particle physics.*

Synonyms: abstruse; arcane; obscure

• •

beliefs or character of a group

*It is the Boy Scouts' **ethos** that one should always be prepared.*

Synonyms: culture; ethic; philosophy

Eulogy
noun
(<u>yoo</u> luh jee)

• •

Euphemism
noun
(<u>yoo</u> fum ih zuhm)

• •

Explicit
adj
(ehk <u>splih</u> siht)

speech in praise of someone

*His best friend gave the **eulogy**, outlining his many achievements and talents.*

Synonyms: commend; extol; laud

• •

use of an inoffensive word or phrase in place of a more distasteful one

*The funeral director preferred to use the **euphemism** "sleeping" instead of the word "dead."*

Synonym: nice-nellyism

• •

clearly stated or shown; forthright in expression

*In Reading Comprehension, questions that ask directly about a detail in the passage are sometimes called **Explicit** Text questions.*

Synonyms: candid; clear-cut; definite; definitive; express; frank; specific; straightforward; unambiguous; unequivocal

Fallow
noun
(<u>faa</u> loh)

· ·

Fanatical
adj
(fuh <u>nah</u> tih kuhl)

· ·

Frugality
noun
(fru <u>gaa</u> luh tee)

dormant; unused

> *This field should lie **fallow** for a year so the soil does not become completely depleted.*

Synonyms: idle; inactive; unseeded

• •

acting excessively enthusiastic; filled with extreme, unquestioned devotion

> *The stormtroopers were **fanatical** in their devotion to the Emperor, readily sacrificing their lives for him.*

Synonyms: extremist; fiery; frenzied; zealous

• •

tending to be thrifty or cheap

> *Scrooge McDuck's **frugality** was so great that he accumulated enough wealth to fill a giant storehouse with money.*

Synonyms: economical; parsimony; prudence; sparing

Gestation
noun
(jeh <u>stay</u> shuhn)

· ·

Gregarious
adj
(greh <u>gayr</u> ee uhs)

· ·

Grievous
adj
(<u>gree</u> vuhs)

growth process from conception to birth

> *The longer the **gestation** period of an organism, the more developed the baby is at birth.*

Synonyms: development; gravidity; pregnancy

• •

outgoing; sociable

> *She was so **gregarious** that when she found herself alone she felt quite sad.*

Synonyms: affable; communicative; congenial; sociable

• •

causing grief or sorrow; serious and distressing

> *Maude and Bertha sobbed loudly throughout the **grievous** event.*

Synonyms: dire; dolorous; grave; mournful

Grovel
verb
(<u>grah</u> vuhl)

. . . .

Gullible
adj
(<u>guh</u> luh buhl)

. . . .

Hegemony
noun
(hih <u>jeh</u> muh nee)

to humble oneself in a demeaning way

*Thor **groveled** to his ex-girlfriend, hoping she would take him back.*

Synonyms: bootlick; cringe; fawn; kowtow; toady

• •

easily deceived

*The con man pretended to be a bank officer so as to fool **gullible** bank customers into giving him their account information.*

Synonyms: credulous; exploitable; naïve

• •

the domination of one state or group over its allies

*When Germany claimed **hegemony** over Russia, Stalin was outraged.*

Synonyms: authority; power

Hermetic
adj
(huhr <u>meh</u> tihk)

. . . .

Heterogenous
adj
(heh tuh ruh <u>jee</u> nee uhs) (he truh <u>jee</u> nyuhs)

. . . .

Homogenous
adj
(huh <u>mah</u> juhn uhs)

tightly sealed

> The **hermetic** seal of the jar proved impossible to break.

Synonyms: airtight; impervious; watertight

• •

composed of unlike parts; different; diverse

> The United Nations is by nature a **heterogeneous** body.

Synonyms: assorted; miscellaneous; mixed; motley; varied

• •

of a similar kind

> The class was fairly **homogenous** since almost all of the students were journalism majors.

Synonyms: consistent; standardized; uniform; unvarying

Hyperbole
noun
(hie <u>puhr</u> boh lee)

· ·

Imbue
verb
(ihm <u>byoo</u>)

· ·

Impasse
noun
(ihm <u>paas</u>) (ihm <u>pass</u>)

purposeful exaggeration for effect

> *When the mayor claimed his town was one of the seven wonders of the world, outsiders classified his statement as a **hyperbole**.*

Synonyms: embellishment; inflation; magnification

· ·

to infuse

> *Marcia struggled to **imbue** her children with decent values, a difficult task in this day and age.*

Synonyms: charge; freight; impregnate; permeate; pervade

· ·

blocked path; dilemma with no solution

> *The rock slide produced an **impasse**, so no one could proceed further on the road.*

Synonyms: cul-de-sac; deadlock; stalemate

Impervious
adj
(ihm <u>puhr</u> vee uhs)

. . . .

Ingenuous
adj
(ihn <u>jehn</u> yoo uhs)

. . . .

Ingrate
noun
(<u>ihn</u> grayt)

impossible to penetrate; incapable of being affected

*A good raincoat will be **impervious** to moisture.*

Synonyms: impregnable; resistant

• •

showing innocence or childlike simplicity

*She was so **ingenuous** that her friends feared her innocence and trustfulness would be exploited when she visited the big city.*

Synonyms: artless; guileless; innocent; naïve; simple; unaffected

• •

ungrateful person

*When none of her relatives thanked her for the fruitcakes she had sent them, Audrey condemned them all as **ingrates**.*

Synonyms: cad; churl

Ingratiate
verb
(ihn <u>gray</u> shee ayt)

. . . .

Innocuous
adj
(ih <u>nahk</u> yoo uhs)

. . . .

Inquest
noun
(<u>ihn</u> kwehst)

to gain favor with another by deliberate effort; to seek to please somebody so as to gain an advantage

> *The new intern tried to **ingratiate** herself with the managers so that they might consider her for a future job.*

Synonyms: curry favor; flatter

• •

harmless

> *Some snakes are poisonous, but most species are **innocuous** and pose no danger to humans.*

Synonyms: benign; harmless; inoffensive; insipid

• •

an investigation; an inquiry

> *The police chief ordered an **inquest** to determine what went wrong.*

Synonyms: probe; quest; research

Insurrection
noun
(ihn suh <u>rehk</u> shuhn)

· ·

Intractable
adj
(Ihn <u>traak</u> tuh buhl)

· ·

Intransigent
adj
(ihn <u>traan</u> suh juhnt) (ihn <u>traan</u> zuh juhnt)

rebellion

> *After the Emperor's troops crushed the **insurrection**, its leaders fled the country.*

Synonyms: mutiny; revolt; revolution; uprising

. . . .

not easily managed or manipulated

> ***Intractable** for hours, the wild horse eventually allowed the rider to mount.*

Synonyms: stubborn; unruly

. . . .

uncompromising; refusing to be reconciled

> *The professor was **intransigent** on the deadline, insisting that everyone turn the assignment in at the same time.*

Synonyms: implacable; inexorable; irreconcilable; obdurate; obstinate; remorseless; rigid; unbending; unrelenting; unyielding

Intrepid
adj
(ihn <u>treh</u> pihd)

. . . .

Inundate
verb
(<u>ih</u> nuhn dayt)

. . . .

Invective
noun
(ihn <u>vek</u> tihv)

fearless, resolutely courageous

*Despite freezing winds, the **intrepid** hiker completed his ascent.*

Synonym: brave

. . . .

to overwhelm, to cover with water

*The tidal wave **inundated** Atlantis, which was lost beneath the water.*

Synonyms: deluge; drown; engulf; flood; submerge

. . . .

abusive language

*A stream of **invectives** poured from Mrs. Pratt's mouth as she watched the vandals smash her ceramic frog.*

Synonyms: denunciation; revilement; vituperation

Itinerant
adj
(ie <u>tihn</u> uhr uhnt)

. . . .

Jargon
noun
(<u>jahr</u> guhn)

. . . .

Jettison
verb
(<u>jeht</u> ih zuhn) (<u>jeht</u> ih suhn)

wandering from place to place; unsettled

> *The **itinerant** tomcat came back to the Johansson homestead every two months.*

Synonyms: nomadic; vagrant

• •

nonsensical talk; specialized language

> *You need to master technical **jargon** in order to communicate successfully with engineers.*

Synonyms: argot; cant; dialect; idiom; slang

• •

to discard; to get rid of as unnecessary or encumbering

> *The sinking ship **jettisoned** its cargo in a desperate attempt to reduce its weight.*

Synonyms: dump; eject

Judicious
adj
(joo <u>dih</u> shuhs)

. . . .

Keen
adj
(keen)

. . . .

Kindle
verb
(<u>kihn</u> duhl)

sensible; showing good judgment

> *The wise and distinguished judge was well known for having a **judicious** temperament.*

Synonyms: circumspect; prudent; sagacious; sapient

. . . .

having a sharp edge; intellectually sharp; perceptive

> *With her **keen** intelligence, she figured out the puzzle in seconds flat.*

Synonyms: acute; canny; quick

. . . .

to set fire to or ignite; excite or inspire

> *With only damp wood to work with, Tilda had great difficulty trying to **kindle** the camp fire.*

Synonyms: arouse; awaken; light; spark

Knell
noun
(nehl)

· ·

Lament
verb
(luh <u>mehnt</u>)

· ·

Larceny
noun
(<u>laar</u> suh nee)

sound of a funeral bell; omen of death or failure

> *When the townspeople heard the **knell** from the church belfry, they knew that their mayor had died.*

Synonyms: chime; peal; toll

· ·

to express sorrow; to grieve

> *The children continued to **lament** the death of the goldfish weeks after its demise.*

Synonyms: bewail; deplore; grieve; mourn

· ·

theft of property

> *The crime of stealing a wallet can be categorized as petty **larceny**.*

Synonyms: burglary; robbery; stealing

Latent
adj
(<u>lay</u> tnt)

· ·

Lavish
adj
(<u>laa</u> vish)

· ·

Leery
adj
(<u>lihr</u> ree)

potential that is not readily apparent

> *Latent* trait testing seeks to identify skills that the test taker may have that they are not aware of.

Synonyms: concealed; dormant; inert; potential; quiescent

. . . .

extremely generous or extravagant; to give unsparingly

> *She was so **lavish** with her puppy that it soon became overweight and spoiled.*

Synonyms: bestow; confer; extravagant; exuberant; luxuriant; opulent; prodigal; profuse; superabundant

. . . .

suspicious

> *After being swindled once, Ruth became **leery** of strangers trying to sell things to her.*

Synonyms: distrustful; guarded; wary

Lethargic
adj
(luh <u>thar</u> jik)

• •

Liberal
adj
(<u>lihb</u> uh ruhl) (<u>lihb</u> ruhl)

• •

Listless
adj
(<u>lihst</u> lihs)

acting in an indifferent or slow, sluggish manner

> *The clerk was so **lethargic** that, even when business was slow, he always had a long line in front of him.*

Synonyms: apathetic; lackadaisical; languid; listless; torpid

. . . .

tolerant; broad-minded; generous; lavish

> *Cali's **liberal** parents trusted her and allowed her to manage her own affairs to a large extent.*

Synonyms: bounteous; latitudinarian; munificent; permissive; progressive

. . . .

lacking energy and enthusiasm

> ***Listless** and depressed after breaking up with his girlfriend, Raj spent his days moping on the couch.*

Synonyms: fainéant; indolent; languid; lethargic; sluggish

Lucid
adj
(<u>loo</u> sihd)

. . . .

Luminous
adj
(<u>loo</u> muhn uhs)

. . . .

Malleable
adj
(<u>mah</u> lee uh buhl) (<u>mal</u> yuh buhl) (<u>mah</u> luh buhl)

clear and easily understood

*The explanations were written in a simple and **lucid** manner so that students were immediately able to apply what they learned.*

Synonyms: clear; coherent; explicit; intelligible; limpid

• •

bright; brilliant; glowing

*The park was bathed in **luminous** sunshine that warmed the bodies and the souls of the visitors.*

Synonyms: incandescent; lucent; lustrous; radiant; resplendent

• •

capable of being shaped

*Gold is the most **malleable** of precious metals; it can easily be formed into almost any shape.*

Synonyms: adaptable; ductile; plastic; pliable; pliant

Meticulous
adj
(mih <u>tihk</u> yuh luhs)

· ·

Monotony
noun
(muh <u>naht</u> nee)

· ·

Naïve
adj
(nah <u>eev</u>)

extremely careful; fastidious; painstaking

*To find all the clues at the crime scene, the **meticulous** investigators examined every inch of the area.*

Synonyms: finicky; fussy; picky; precise; punctilious; scrupulous

• •

no variation; tediously the same

*The **monotony** of the sound of the dripping faucet almost drove the research assistant crazy.*

Synonyms: drone; tedium

• •

lacking sophistication or experience

*Inexperienced writers often are **naïve** and assume that big words make them sound smarter.*

Synonyms: artless; credulous; guileless; ingenuous; simple; unaffected; unsophisticated

Nascent
adj
(<u>nay</u> sehnt)

· ·

Nuance
noun
(<u>noo</u> ahns)

· ·

Obstinate
adj
(<u>ahb</u> stih nuht)

starting to develop; coming into existence

> *The advertising campaign was still in a **nascent** stage, and nothing had been finalized yet.*

Synonyms: embryonic; emerging; inchoate; incipient

. . . .

a subtle expression of meaning or quality

> *The scholars argued for hours over tiny **nuances** in the interpretation of the last line of the poem.*

Synonyms: gradation; subtlety; tone

. . . .

stubborn; unyielding

> *The **obstinate** child could not be made to eat any food that he perceived to be "yucky."*

Synonyms: intransigent; mulish; persistent; pertinacious; stubborn; tenacious

Overwrought
adj
(oh vuhr <u>rawt</u>)

. . . .

Palatial
adj
(puh <u>lay</u> shuhl)

. . . .

Panache
noun
(puh <u>nahsh</u>)

agitated; overdone

> *The lawyer's **overwrought** voice on the phone made her clients worry about the outcome of their case.*

Synonyms: elaborate; excited; nervous; ornate

• •

relating to a palace; magnificent

> *After living in a cramped studio apartment for years, Siobhan thought the modest one bedroom looked down-right **palatial**.*

Synonyms: grand; stately

• •

flamboyance or dash in style and action; verve

> *Leah has such **panache** when planning parties, even when they're last-minute affairs.*

Synonym: flair

Paradox
noun
(<u>par</u> uh doks)

• •

Pariah
noun
(puh <u>rie</u> uh)

• •

Pejorative
noun
(<u>peh</u> jaw ruh tihv)

a contradiction or dilemma

*It is a **paradox** that those most in need of medical attention are often those least able to obtain it.*

Synonyms: ambiguity; incongruity

• •

an outcast

*Once he betrayed those in his community, he was banished and lived the life of a **pariah**.*

Synonyms: castaway; derelict; leper; offscouring; untouchable

• •

having bad connotations; disparaging

*The teacher scolded Mark for his unduly **pejorative** comments about his classmate's presentation.*

Synonyms: belittling; dismissive; insulting

Permeate
verb
(<u>puhr</u> mee ayt)

. . . .

Pervade
verb
(puhr <u>vayd</u>)

. . . .

Phalanx
noun
(<u>fay</u> laanks)

to penetrate

> *This miraculous new cleaning fluid is able to **permeate** stains and dissolve them in minutes!*

Synonyms: imbue; infuse; pervade; suffuse

• •

to be present throughout; to permeate

> *Four spices—cumin, turmeric, coriander and cayenne— **pervade** almost every Indian dish, and give the cuisine its distinctive flavor.*

Synonyms: imbue; infuse; penetrate; permeate; suffuse

• •

a compact or close-knit body of people, animals, or things

> *A **phalanx** of guards stood outside the prime minister's home day and night.*

Synonyms: legion; mass

Philanthropy
noun
(fihl <u>aan</u> throh pee)

. . . .

Philistine
noun
(<u>fihl</u> uh steen)

. . . .

Placate
verb
(<u>play</u> cayt)

charity; a desire or effort to promote goodness

> *The Metropolitan Museum of Art owes much of its collection to the **philanthropy** of private collectors who willed their estates to the museum.*

Synonyms: altruism; humanitarianism

. . . .

a person who is guided by materialism and is disdainful of intellectual or artistic values

> *The **philistine** never even glanced at the rare violin in his collection but instead kept an eye on its value and sold it at a profit.*

Synonyms: boor; bourgeois; capitalist; clown; lout; materialist; vulgarian

. . . .

to soothe or pacify

> *The burglar tried to **placate** the snarling dog by referring to it as a 'Nice Doggy' and offering it a treat.*

Synonyms: appease; conciliate; mollify

Plethora
noun
(<u>pleh</u> thor uh)

. . . .

Plucky
adj
(<u>pluh</u> kee)

. . . .

Polemic
noun
(puh <u>leh</u> mihk)

excess

*Assuming that more was better, the defendant offered the judge a **plethora** of excuses.*

Synonyms: glut; overabundance; superfluity; surfeit

• •

courageous; spunky

*The **plucky** young nurse dove into the foxhole, determined to help the wounded soldier.*

Synonyms: brave; bold; gutsy

• •

controversy; argument; verbal attack

*The candidate's **polemic** against his opponent was vicious and small-minded rather than convincing and well-reasoned.*

Synonyms: denunciation; refutation

Posit
verb
(<u>pah</u> siht)

• •

Pragmatic
adj
(praag <u>maa</u> tihk)

• •

Pristine
adj
(prih <u>steen</u>)

to assume as real or conceded; propose as an explanation

*Before proving the math formula, we needed to **posit** that x and y were real numbers.*

Synonym: suggest

. . . .

practical, as opposed to idealistic

*While idealistic gamblers think they can get rich by frequenting casinos, **pragmatic** gamblers realize that the odds are heavily stacked against them.*

Synonyms: rational; realistic

. . . .

fresh and clean; uncorrupted

*Since concerted measures had been taken to prevent looting, the archeological site was still **pristine** when researchers arrived.*

Synonyms: innocent; undamaged

Prodigal
adj
(<u>prah</u> dih guhl)

· ·

Proliferate
verb
(proh <u>lih</u> fuhr ayt)

· ·

Prudence
noun
(<u>proo</u> dehns)

lavish; wasteful

> *The **prodigal** son quickly wasted all of his inheritance on a lavish lifestyle devoted to pleasure.*

Synonyms: extravagant; lavish; profligate; spendthrift; wasteful

• •

to increase in number quickly

> *Although he only kept two guinea pigs initially, they **proliferated** to such an extent that he soon had dozens.*

Synonyms: breed; multiply; procreate; propagate; reproduce; spawn

• •

wisdom; caution or restraint

> *The college student exhibited **prudence** by obtaining practical experience along with her studies, which greatly strengthened her resume.*

Synonyms: astuteness; circumspection; discretion; frugality; judiciousness; providence; thrift

Pungent
adj
(<u>puhn</u> juhnt)

· ·

Quotidian
adj
(kwo <u>tih</u> dee uhn)

· ·

Repast
noun
(<u>rih</u> paast)

sharp and irritating to the senses

*The smoke from the burning tires was extremely **pungent**.*

Synonyms: acrid; caustic; piquant; poignant; stinging

• •

occurring daily; commonplace

*The sight of people singing on the street is so **quotidian** in New York that passersby rarely react to it.*

Synonyms: everyday; normal; usual

• •

meal or mealtime

*Ravi prepared a delicious **repast** of chicken tikka and naan.*

Synonyms: banquet; feast

Repose
noun
(rih <u>pohz</u>)

. . . .

Repudiate
verb
(ree <u>pyoo</u> dee ayt)

. . . .

Rhetoric
noun
(<u>reh</u> tuhr ihk)

relaxation; leisure

*After working hard every day in the busy city, Mike finds his **repose** on weekends playing golf with friends.*

Synonyms: calmness; tranquility

. . . .

to reject the validity of

*The old woman's claim that she was Russian royalty was **repudiated** when DNA tests showed she was of no relation to them.*

Synonyms: deny; disavow; disclaim; disown; renounce

. . . .

effective writing or speaking

*Lincoln's talent for **rhetoric** was evident in his beautifully expressed Gettysburg Address.*

Synonyms: eloquence; oratory

Rustic
adj
(<u>ruh</u> stihk)

. . . .

Sentient
adj
(<u>sehn</u> shuhnt)

. . . .

Slake
verb
(slayk)

rural

> *The **rustic** cabin was an ideal setting for a vacation in the country.*

Synonyms: bucolic; pastoral

• •

aware; conscious; able to perceive

> *The anesthetic didn't work, and I was still **sentient** when the dentist started drilling!*

Synonyms: feeling; intelligent; thinking

• •

to calm down or moderate

> *In order to **slake** his curiosity, Bryan finally took a tour backstage at the theater.*

Synonyms: moderate; quench; satisfy

Sportive
adj
(<u>spohr</u> tihv)

· ·

Stasis
noun
(<u>stay</u> sihs)

· ·

Stigma
noun
(<u>stihg</u> mah)

frolicsome; playful

> *The lakeside vacation meant more **sportive** opportunities for the kids than the wine tour through France.*

Synonyms: frisky; merry

. . . .

a state of static balance or equilibrium; stagnation

> *The rusty, ivy-covered World War II tank had obviously been in **stasis** for years.*

Synonyms: inertia; standstill

. . . .

a mark of shame or discredit

> *In* The Scarlet Letter *Hester Prynne was required to wear the letter 'A' on her clothes as a public **stigma** for her adultery.*

Synonyms: blemish; blot; opprobrium; stain; taint

Stratagem
noun
(<u>straa</u> tuh juhm)

· ·

Sully
verb
(<u>suh</u> lee)

· ·

Supplant
verb
(suh <u>plaant</u>)

trick designed to deceive an enemy

*The Trojan Horse must be one of the most successful military **stratagems** used throughout history.*

Synonyms: artifice; feint; maneuver; ruse; while

· ·

to tarnish; to taint

*With the help of a public relations firm, he was able to restore his **sullied** reputation.*

Synonyms: besmirch; defile

· ·

to replace (another) by force; to take the place of

*The overthrow of the government meant a new leader to **supplant** the tyrannical former one.*

Synonyms: displace; supersede

Surly
adj
(<u>suhr</u> lee)

• •

Symbiosis
noun
(ɜihm bee <u>oh</u> sihs)

• •

Tangential
adj
(taan <u>jehn</u> shuhl)

rude and bad-tempered

> *When asked to clean the windshield, the **surly** gas station attendant tossed a dirty rag at the customer and walked away.*

Synonyms: gruff; grumpy; testy

• •

cooperation; mutual helpfulness

> *The rhino and the tick-eating bird live in **symbiosis**; the rhino gives the bird food in the form of ticks, and the bird rids the rhino of parasites.*

Synonyms: association; interdependence

• •

digressing; diverting

> *Your argument is interesting, but it's **tangential** to the matter at hand, so I suggest we get back to the point.*

Synonyms: digressive; extraneous; inconsequential; irrelevant; peripheral

Terrestrial
adj
(tuh <u>reh</u> stree uhl)

· ·

Tirade
noun
(<u>tie</u> rayd)

· ·

Tome
noun
(tohm)

earthly; down-to-earth; commonplace

> *Many "extraterrestrial" objects turn out to be **terrestrial** in origin, as when flying saucers turn out to be normal airplanes.*

Synonyms: earthbound; mundane; sublunary; tellurian; terrene

• •

long, harsh speech or verbal attack

> *Observers were shocked at the manager's **tirade** over such a minor mistake.*

Synonyms: diatribe; fulmination; harangue; obloquy; revilement; vilification

• •

book, usually large and academic

> *The teacher was forced to refer to various **tomes** to find the answer to the advanced student's question.*

Synonyms: codex; volume

Transitory
adj
(<u>trahn</u> sih tohr ee)

. . . .

Unconscionable
adj
(uhn <u>kahn</u> shuhn uh buhl)

. . . .

Unequivocal
adj
(uhn ee <u>kwih</u> vih kuhl)

temporary; lasting a brief time

> *The reporter lived a **transitory** life, staying in one place only long enough to cover the current story.*

Synonyms: ephemeral; evanescent; fleeting; impermanent; momentary

• •

unscrupulous; shockingly unfair or unjust

> *After she promised me the project, the fact that she gave it to someone else is **unconscionable**.*

Synonyms: dishonorable; indefensible

• •

absolute; certain

> *The jury's verdict was **unequivocal**: the organized crime boss would be locked up for life.*

Synonyms: categorical; clear; explicit; express; unambiguous

Vacillate
verb
(<u>vaa</u> sihl ayt)

. . . .

Venerable
adj
(<u>veh</u> nehr uh buhl)

. . . .

Venerate
verb
(<u>vehn</u> uhr ayt)

to physically sway; to be indecisive

> *The customer held up the line as he **vacillated** between ordering chocolate-chip or rocky-road ice cream.*

Synonyms: dither; falter; fluctuate; oscillate; waver

• •

respected because of age

> *All of the villagers sought the **venerable** old woman's advice whenever they had a problem.*

Synonyms: distinguished; elderly; respectable

• •

to respect deeply

> *In a traditional Confucian society the young **venerate** their elders, deferring to the elders' wisdom and experience.*

Synonyms: adore; honor; idolize; revere

Veracity
noun
(vuhr <u>aa</u> sih tee)

. . . .

Verbose
adj
(vuhr <u>bohs</u>)

. . . .

Vestige
noun
(<u>veh</u> stihj)

filled with truth and accuracy

> *She had a reputation for **veracity**, so everyone trusted her description of events.*

Synonyms: candor; exactitude; fidelity; probity

• •

wordy

> *The professor's answer was so **verbose** that his student forgot what the original question had been.*

Synonyms: longwinded; loquacious; prolix; superfluous

• •

a trace; remnant

> ***Vestiges** of the former tenant still remained in the apartment, though he hadn't lived there for years.*

Synonyms: relic; remains; sign

Volatile
adj
(<u>vah</u> luh tuhl)

• •

Waver
verb
(<u>way</u> vuhr)

• •

Whimsical
adj
(<u>wihm</u> sih cuhl)

easily aroused or changeable; lively or explosive

*His **volatile** personality made it difficult to predict his reaction to anything.*

Synonyms: capricious; erratic; fickle; inconsistent; inconstant; mercurial; temperamental

• •

to fluctuate between choices

*If you **waver** too long before making a decision about which testing site to register for, you may not get your first choice.*

Synonyms: dither; falter; fluctuate; oscillate; vacillate; waver

• •

lightly acting in a fanciful or capricious manner; unpredictable

*The ballet was **whimsical**, delighting the children with its imaginative characters and unpredictable sets.*

Synonyms: capricious; erratic; flippant; frivolous

Wily
adj
(<u>wie</u> lee)

· ·

Wraith
noun
(rayth)

· ·

Zeal
adj
(zeehl)

clever; deceptive

> *Yet again, the **wily** coyote managed to elude the ranchers who wanted to capture it.*

Synonyms: crafty; cunning; tricky

. . . .

a ghost or specter; a ghost of a living person seen just before his or her death

> *Gideon thought he saw a wraith late one night as he sat **vigil** outside his great uncle's bedroom door.*

Synonyms: apparition; bogeyman; phantasm; shade; spirit

. . . .

passion; excitement

> *She brought her typical **zeal** to the project, sparking enthusiasm in the other team members.*

Synonyms: ardency; fervor; fire; passion

Zenith
noun
(<u>zee</u> nihth)

. . . .

Accretion
noun
(uh <u>kree</u> shuhn)

. . . .

Aggrandize
verb
(uh <u>graan</u> diez) (<u>aa</u> gruhn diez)

the point of culmination; peak

> *The diva considered her appearance at the Metropolitan Opera to be the **zenith** of her career.*

Synonyms: acme; pinnacle

. . . .

a growth in size; an increase in amount

> *The committee's strong fund-raising efforts resulted in an **accretion** in scholarship money.*

Synonyms: accumulation; buildup

. . . .

to increase in power, influence and reputation

> *The supervisor sought to **aggrandize** himself by claiming that the achievements of his staff were actually his own.*

Synonyms: amplify; apotheosize; augment; dignify; elevate; enlarge; ennoble; exalt; glorify; magnify; swell; uplift; wax

Anomaly
noun
(uh <u>nahm</u> uh lee)

· ·

Ameliorate
verb
(uh <u>meel</u> yuhr ayt)

· ·

Analgesia
noun
(aah nuhl <u>jee</u> zhuh)

deviation from what is normal

*Albino animals may display too great an **anomaly** in their coloring to attract normally colored mates.*

Synonyms: aberrant; aberration; abnormality; deviance; deviation; irregularity; preternaturalness

• •

to make better; to improve

*The doctor was able to **ameliorate** the patient's suffering using painkillers.*

Synonyms: amend; better; improve; pacify; upgrade

• •

a lessening of pain without loss of consciousness

*After having her appendix removed, Tatiana welcomed the **analgesia** that the painkillers provided.*

Apocryphal
adj
(uh <u>pahk</u> ruh fuhl)

· ·

Apostate
noun
(uh <u>pahs</u> tayt)

· ·

Ardor
noun
(<u>ahr</u> duhr)

of questionable authority or authenticity

*There is no hard or authoritative evidence to support the **apocryphal** tales that link the Roswell, New Mexico incident to a downed U.F.O.*

Synonyms: disputed; doubtful; fictitious; fraudulent

• •

one who renounces a religious faith

*So that he could divorce his wife, the king scoffed at the church doctrines and declared himself an **apostate**.*

Synonyms: defector; deserter; traitor

• •

intense and passionate feeling

*Bishop's **ardor** for landscape was evident when he passionately described the beauty of the scenic Hudson Valley.*

Synonyms: devotion; enthusiasm; enthusiasm; fervency; fervidity; fervidness; fervor; fire; passion; zeal; zealousness

Attenuate
verb
(uh <u>tehn</u> yoo ayt)

· ·

August
adj
(aw <u>guhst</u>)

· ·

Bevy
noun
(<u>beh</u> vee)

reduce in force or degree; weaken

> *The Bill of Rights **attenuated** the traditional power of government to change laws at will.*

Synonyms: debilitate; devitalize; dilute; enervate; enfeeble; rarefy; sap; thin; undermine; undo; unnerve; water; weaken

• •

dignified; grandiose

> *The **august** view of the Grand Teton summit took my breath away.*

Synonyms: admirable; awesome; grand; majestic

• •

group

> *As predicted, a **bevy** of teenagers surrounded the rock star's limousine.*

Synonyms: band; bunch; gang; pack; troop

Bifurcate
verb
(<u>bi</u> fuhr kayt) (bi <u>fuhr</u> kayt)

· ·

Blight
verb
(bliet)

· ·

Blithe
adj
(blieth)

divide into two parts

> *The large corporation just released a press statement announcing its plans to **bifurcate**.*

Synonym: bisect

. . . .

to afflict; to destroy

> *The farmers feared that the night's frost would **blight** the potato crops entirely.*

Synonyms: damage; plague

. . . .

joyful; cheerful; without appropriate thought

> *Summer finally came, and the **blithe** students spent their days at the beach.*

Synonyms: carefree; lighthearted; merry

Bolster
verb
(<u>bohl</u> stuhr)

• •

Cabal
noun
(kuh <u>bahl</u>)

• •

Cacophony
noun
(kuh <u>kah</u> fuh nee)

support; prop up

> *The presence of giant footprints **bolstered** the argument that Bigfoot was in the area.*

Synonyms: brace; buttress; crutch; prop; stay; support; sustain; underpinning; uphold

. . . .

a secret group seeking to overturn something

> *The boys on the street formed a **cabal** to keep girls out of their tree house.*

Synonyms: camp; circle; clan; clique; coterie; in-group; mafia; mob; ring

. . . .

harsh, jarring noise

> *The junior high orchestra created an almost unbearable **cacophony** as they tried to tune their instruments.*

Synonyms: chaos; clamor; din; discord; disharmony; noise

Candid
adj
(<u>kaan</u> did)

· ·

Cartography
noun
(kahr <u>tahg</u> ruh fee)

· ·

Castigate
verb
(<u>kaa</u> stih gayt)

impartial and honest in speech

> *The observations of a child can be charming since they are **candid** and unpretentious.*

Synonyms: direct; forthright; frank; honest; open; sincere; straight; straightforward; undisguised

. . . .

science or art of making maps

> *Gail's interest in **cartography** may stem from the extensive traveling she did as a child.*

Synonyms: charting; surveying; topography

. . . .

to punish or criticize harshly

> *Martina **castigated** her boyfriend for not remembering her birthday.*

Synonyms: admonish; chastise; chide; rebuke; reprimand; reproach; reprove; scold; tax; upbraid

Caustic
adj
(<u>kah</u> stihk)

. . . .

Chauvinist
noun
(<u>shoh</u> vuh nist)

. . . .

Cloying
adj
(<u>kloy</u> ing)

biting in wit

*Dorothy Parker gained her **caustic** reputation from her cutting, yet witty, insults.*

Synonyms: acerbic; biting; mordant; trenchant

. . . .

someone prejudiced in favor of a group to which he or she belongs

*The attitude that men must be obeyed since they are inherently superior to women is common among male **chauvinists**.*

Synonyms: biased; colored; one-sided; partial; partisan; prejudicial; prepossessed; tendentious

. . . .

sickly sweet; excessive

*When Enid and Jay first started dating, their **cloying** affection towards one another often made their friends ill.*

Synonyms: excessive; fulsome

Coffer
noun
(<u>kah</u> fuhr)

• •

Collusion
noun
(kuh <u>loo</u> zhuhn)

• •

Condone
verb
(kuhn <u>dohn</u>)

strongbox; large chest for money

> *The bulletproof glass of the **coffer** is what keeps the crown jewels secure.*

Synonyms: treasury, chest, exchequer, war chest

• •

collaboration; complicity; conspiracy

> *It came to light that the police chief and the mafia had a **collusion** in running the numbers racket.*

Synonyms: connivance; intrigue; machination

• •

to overlook, pardon, or disregard

> *Some theorists believe that failing to prosecute minor crimes is the same as **condoning** an air of lawlessness.*

Synonyms: exculpate; excuse; pardon; remit

Harder

Contrite
adj
(kuhn triet)

• •

Craven
adj
(kray vuhn)

• •

Credulous
adj
(kreh juh luhs)

deeply sorrowful and repentant for a wrong

*After three residents were mugged in the lobby while the watchman was away from his post, he felt very **contrite**.*

Synonyms: apologetic; regretful; remorseful

· ·

lacking courage

*The **craven** lion cringed in the corner of his cage, terrified of the mouse.*

Synonyms: faint-hearted; spineless; timid

· ·

too trusting; gullible

*Although some 4-year-olds believe in the Tooth Fairy, only the most **credulous** 9-year-olds also believe in her.*

Synonyms: naïve; susceptible; trusting

Curmudgeon
noun
(kuhr <u>muh</u> juhn)

. . . .

Decorous
adj
(<u>deh</u> kuhr uhs) (deh <u>kohr</u> uhs)

. . . .

Decorum
noun
(deh <u>kohr</u> uhm)

cranky person, usually old

*Ernesto was a notorious **curmudgeon** who snapped at anyone who disturbed him for any reason.*

Synonyms: crab; coot; grouch

. . . .

proper; tasteful; socially correct

*The countess trained her daughters in the finer points of **decorous** behavior, hoping they would make a good impression when she presented them at Court.*

Synonyms: appropriate; comme il faut; courteous; polite

. . . .

appropriateness of behavior or conduct; propriety

*The countess complained that the vulgar peasants lacked the **decorum** appropriate for a visit to the palace.*

Synonyms: correctness; decency; etiquette; manners; mores; propriety; seemliness

Demur
verb
(dih <u>muhr</u>)

. . . .

Deride
verb
(dih <u>ried</u>)

. . . .

Desiccate
verb
(<u>deh</u> sih kayt)

to express doubts or objections

*When scientific authorities claimed that all the planets revolved around the Earth, Galileo, with his superior understanding of the situation, was forced to **demur**.*

Synonyms: dissent; expostulate; kick; protest; remonstrate

• •

to speak of or treat with contempt, to mock

*The awkward child was often **derided** by his "cooler" peers.*

Synonyms: gibe; jeer; mock; ridicule; scoff; sneer taunt

• •

to dry out thoroughly

*After a few weeks lying on the desert's baking sands the cow's carcass became completely **desiccated**.*

Synonyms: dehydrate; dry; parch

Diatribe
noun
(<u>die</u> uh trieb)

. . . .

Dictum
noun
(<u>dihk</u> tuhm)

. . . .

Dissemble
verb
(dihs <u>sehm</u> buhl)

an abusive, condemnatory speech

> *The trucker bellowed a **diatribe** at the driver who had cut him off.*

Synonyms: fulmination; harangue; invective; jeremiad; malediction; obloquy; tirade

• •

authoritative statement

> *"You have time to lean, you have time to clean," was the **dictum** our boss made us live by.*

Synonyms: adage; apothegm; aphorism; decree; edict

• •

to present a false appearance; to disguise one's real intentions or character

> *The villain could **dissemble** to the police no longer—he admitted the deed and tore up the floor to reveal the stash of stolen money.*

Synonyms: act; affect; assume; camouflage; cloak; counterfeit; cover up; disguise; dissimulate; fake; feign; mask; masquerade; pose; pretend; put on; sham

Dissonance
noun
(<u>dihs</u> uh nuhns)

• •

Distend
verb
(dih <u>stehnd</u>)

• •

Doctrinaire
adj
(dahk truh <u>nayr</u>)

a harsh and disagreeable combination, especially of sounds

> *Cognitive **dissonance** is the inner conflict produced when long-standing beliefs are contradicted by new evidence.*

Synonyms: clash; contention; discord; dissension; dissent; dissidence; friction; strife; variance

. . . .

to swell; to inflate; to bloat

> *Her stomach was **distended** after she gorged on the six-course meal.*

Synonyms: broaden; bulge

. . . .

rigidly devoted to theories without regard for practicality; dogmatic

> *The professor's manner of teaching was considered **doctrinaire** for such a liberal school.*

Synonyms: dictatorial; inflexible

Droll
adj
(drohl)

. . . .

Dupe
verb
(doop)

. . . .

Ebullient
adj
(ih <u>byool</u> yuhnt) (ih <u>buhl</u> yuhnt)

amusing in a wry, subtle way

> *Although the play couldn't be described as hilarious, it was certainly **droll**.*

Synonyms: comic; entertaining; funny; risible; witty

• •

to deceive or a person who is easily deceived

> *Bugs Bunny was able to **dupe** Elmer Fudd by dressing up as a lady rabbit.*

Synonyms: beguile; betray; bluff; cozen; deceive; delude; fool; hoodwink; humbug; mislead; take in trick

• •

exhilarated, full of enthusiasm and high spirits

> *The **ebullient** child exhausted the baby-sitter, who lacked the energy to keep up with her.*

Synonyms: ardent; avid; bubbly; zestful

Eclectic
adj
(ih <u>klehk</u> tihk) (eh <u>klehk</u> tihk)

. . . .

Efficacy
noun
(<u>eh</u> tih kuh see)

. . . .

Effigy
noun
(<u>eh</u> fuh jee)

selecting from or made up from a variety of sources

> *Budapest's architecture is an **eclectic** mix of eastern and western styles.*

Synonyms: broad; catholic; selective

. . . .

effectiveness

> *The **efficacy** of penicillin was unsurpassed when it was first introduced, completely eliminating almost all bacterial infections.*

Synonyms: dynamism; effectiveness; efficiency; force; power; productiveness; proficiency; strength; vigor

. . . .

stuffed doll; likeness of a person

> *In England, **effigies** of the historic rebel Guy Fawkes are burned in commemoration of his life.*

Synonyms: dummy; figure; image

Emulate
verb
(<u>ehm</u> yuh layt)

· ·

Endemic
adj
(ehn <u>deh</u> mihk)

· ·

Engender
verb
(ehn <u>gehn</u> duhr)

to copy; to try to equal or excel

> *The graduate student sought to **emulate** his professor in every way, copying not only how she taught but also how she conducted herself outside of class.*

Synonyms: ape; imitate; simulate

• •

belonging to a particular area; inherent

> *The health department determined that the outbreak was **endemic** to the small village, so they quarantined the inhabitants before the virus could spread.*

Synonyms: indigenous; local; native

• •

to produce, cause, or bring about

> *His fear and hatred of clowns was **engendered** when he witnessed a bank robbery carried out by five men wearing clown suits and make-up.*

Synonyms: beget; generate; procreate; proliferate; reproduce; spawn

Ephemeral
adj
(ih <u>fehm</u> uhr uhl)

. . . .

Erudite
adj
(<u>ehr</u> yuh dite) (<u>ehr</u> uh dite)

. . . .

Fecund
adj
(<u>fee</u> kuhnd) (<u>feh</u> kuhnd)

lasting a short time

> *The lives of mayflies seem **ephemeral** to us, since the flies' average life span is a matter of hours.*

Synonyms: evanescent; fleeting; momentary; transient

. . . .

learned; scholarly; bookish

> *The annual meeting of philosophy professors was a gathering of the most **erudite**, well-published individuals in the field.*

Synonyms: learned; scholastic; wise

. . . .

fertile; fruitful; productive

> *The **fecund** couple yielded a total of 20 children.*

Synonyms: flourishing; prolific

Fetid
adj
(<u>feh</u> tihd)

· ·

Flag
verb
(flaag)

· ·

Florid
adj
(<u>flohr</u> ihd) (<u>flahr</u> ihd)

foul-smelling; putrid

> *The **fetid** stench from the outhouse caused Francesca to wrinkle her nose in disgust.*

Synonyms: funky; malodorous; noisome; rank; stinky

. . . .

to decline in vigor, strength, or interest

> *The marathon runner slowed down as his strength **flagged**.*

Synonyms: dwindle; ebb; slacken; subside; wane

. . . .

excessively decorated or embellished

> *The palace had been decorated in an excessively **florid** style; every surface had been carved and gilded.*

Synonyms: Baroque; elaborate; flamboyant; ornate; ostentatious; Rococo

Fortuitous
adj
(fohr <u>too</u> ih tuhs)

· ·

Frenetic
adj
(fruh <u>neht</u> ihk)

· ·

Garner
verb
(<u>gahr</u> nuhr)

happening by chance, fortunate

*It was **fortuitous** that he won the lotto just before he had to pay back his loans.*

Synonyms: chance; fortunate; haphazard; lucky; propitious; prosperous

• •

frantic, frenzied

*The employee's **frenetic** schedule left her little time to socialize.*

Synonym: corybantic; delirious; feverish; mad; rabid; wild

• •

to gather and store

*The director managed to **garner** financial backing from several different sources for his next project.*

Synonyms: amass; acquire; glean; harvest; reap

Garrulous
adj
(<u>gaar</u> uh luhs) (<u>gaar</u> yuh luhs)

. . . .

Glower
verb
(<u>glow</u> uhr)

. . . .

Gradation
noun
(gray <u>day</u> shuhn)

tending to talk a lot

> *The **garrulous** parakeet distracted its owner with its continuous talking.*

Synonyms: effusive; loquacious

· ·

to glare; to stare angrily and intensely

> *The cranky waiter **glowered** at the indecisive customer.*

Synonyms: frown; lower; scowl

· ·

process occurring by regular degrees or stages; variation in color

> *The paint store offers so many different **gradations** of red that it's impossible to choose among them.*

Synonyms: nuance; shade; step; subtlety

Guile
noun
(<u>gie</u> uhl)

. . . .

Hoary
adj
(<u>hohr</u> ee) (<u>haw</u> ree)

. . . .

Iconoclast
noun
(ie <u>kahn</u> uh klaast)

deceit, trickery

> *Since he was not fast enough to catch the roadrunner on foot, the coyote resorted to **guile** in an effort to trap his enemy.*

Synonyms: artifice; chicanery; connivery; duplicity

• •

very old; whitish or gray from age

> *The old man's **hoary** beard contrasted starkly to the new stubble of his teenage grandson.*

Synonyms: ancient; antediluvian; antique; venerable; vintage

• •

one who opposes established beliefs, customs and institutions

> *His lack of regard for traditional beliefs soon established him as an **iconoclast**.*

Synonyms: maverick; nonconformist; rebel; revolutionary

Idiosyncracy
noun
(ih dee uh <u>sihn</u> kruh see)

∙ ∙

Impetuous
adj
(ihm <u>peh</u> choo uhs) (ihm <u>pehch</u> wuhs)

∙ ∙

Implacable
adj
(ihm <u>play</u> kuh buhl) (ihm <u>plaa</u> kuh buhl)

peculiarity of temperament; eccentricity

> *His numerous **idiosyncrasies** included a fondness for wearing bright green shoes with mauve socks.*

Synonyms: humor; oddity; quirk

• •

quick to act without thinking

> *It is not good for an investment broker to be **impetuous** since much thought should be given to all the possible options.*

Synonyms: impulsive; precipitate; rash; reckless; spontaneous

• •

unable to be calmed down or made peaceful

> *His rage at the betrayal was so great that he remained **implacable** for weeks.*

Synonyms: inexorable; intransigent; irreconcilable; relentless; remorseless; unforgiving; unrelenting

Inexorable
adj
(ihn <u>ehk</u> suhr uh buhl)

• •

Inter
verb
(ihn <u>tuhr</u>)

• •

Irascible
adj
(ih <u>rah</u> suh buhl)

inflexible; unyielding

> *The **inexorable** force of the twister swept away their house.*

Synonyms: adamant; relentless obdurate

· ·

to bury

> *After giving the masses one last chance to pay their respects, the leader's body was **interred**.*

Synonyms: entomb; inhume; sepulcher; sepulture; tomb

· ·

easily made angry

> *Attilla the Hun's **irascible** and violent nature made all who dealt with him fear for their lives.*

Synonyms: cantankerous; irritable; ornery; testy

Kinetic
adj
(kih <u>neh</u> tihk)

· ·

Laconic
adj
(luh <u>kah</u> nihk)

· ·

Lampoon
verb
(laam <u>poon</u>)

relating to motion; characterized by movement

> *The **kinetic** sculpture moved back and forth, startling the museum visitors.*

Synonyms: active; dynamic; mobile

. . . .

using few words

> *He was the classic **laconic** native of Maine; he talked as if he were being charged for each word.*

Synonyms: concise; curt; pithy; taciturn; terse

. . . .

to ridicule with satire

> *The mayor hated being **lampooned** by the press for his efforts to improve people's politeness.*

Synonym: tease

Languid
adj
(<u>laang</u> gwihd)

. . . .

Lassitude
noun
(<u>laas</u> ih tood)

. . . .

Levity
noun
(<u>leh</u> vih tee)

lacking energy; indifferent; slow

> *The **languid** cat cleaned its fur, ignoring the vicious, snarling dog chained a few feet away from it.*

Synonyms: fainéant; lackadaisical; listless; sluggish; weak

. . . .

a state of diminished energy

> *The lack of energy that characterizes patients with anemia makes **lassitude** one of the primary symptoms of the disease.*

Synonyms: debilitation; enervation; fatigue; languor; listlessness; tiredness; weariness

. . . .

an inappropriate lack of seriousness, overly casual

> *The joke added needed **levity** to the otherwise serious meeting.*

Synonyms: amusement; humor

Libertine
noun
(<u>lihb</u> uhr teen)

• •

Lionize
verb
(<u>lie</u> uhn iez)

• •

Livid
adj
(<u>lih</u> vihd)

a free thinker, usually used disparagingly; one without moral restraint

> *The **libertine** took pleasure in gambling away his family's money.*

Synonym: hedonist

. . . .

to treat as a celebrity

> *After the success of his novel, the author was **lionized** by the press.*

Synonyms: feast; honor; ply; regale

. . . .

reddened with anger

> *André was **livid** when he discovered that someone had spilled grape juice all over his cashmere coat.*

Synonyms: furious; enraged; fuming; incensed

Loquacious
adj
(loh <u>kway</u> shuhs)

· ·

Lumber
verb
(<u>luhm</u> buhr)

· ·

Machination
noun
(mahk uh <u>nay</u> shuhn)

talkative

> *She is naturally **loquacious**, which is a problem in situations where listening is more important than talking.*

Synonyms: effusive; garrulous; verbose

. . . .

to move slowly and awkwardly

> *The bear **lumbered** towards the garbage, drooling at the prospect of the Big Mac leftovers he smelled.*

Synonyms: galumph; hulk; lurch; stumble

. . . .

plot or scheme

> *Tired of his enemies' endless **machinations** to remove him from the throne, the king had them executed.*

Synonyms: cabal; conspiracy; design; intrigue

Maelstrom
noun
(<u>mayl</u> struhm)

• •

Malinger
verb
(muh <u>ling</u> guhr)

• •

Mannered
adj
(<u>maan</u> uhrd)

whirlpool; turmoil; agitated state of mind

*The transportation system of the city had collapsed in the **maelstrom** of war.*

Synonyms: Charybdis; eddy; turbulence

· ·

to evade responsibility by pretending to be ill

*A common way to avoid the draft was by **malingering**— pretending to be mentally or physically ill so as to avoid being taken by the Army.*

Synonyms: shirk; slack

· ·

artificial or stilted in character

*The portrait is an example of the **mannered** style that was favored in that era.*

Synonyms: affected; unnatural

Mar
verb
(mahr)

· ·

Maudlin
adj
(<u>mawd</u> lihn)

· ·

Militate
verb
(<u>mihl</u> ih tayt)

to damage; deface; to spoil

> *Telephone poles **mar** the natural beauty of the country-side.*

Synonyms: blemish; disfigure; impair; injure; scar

• •

overly sentimental

> *The mother's death should have been a touching scene, but the movie's treatment of it was so **maudlin** that, instead of making the audience cry, it made them cringe.*

Synonyms: bathetic; mawkish; saccharine; weepy

• •

to operate against, work against

> *Lenin **militated** against the tsar for years before he over-threw him and established the Soviet Union.*

Synonyms: influence; affect; change

Misanthrope
noun
(<u>mihs</u> ahn throhp)

· ·

Missive
noun
(<u>mihs</u> ihv)

· ·

Mollify
verb
(<u>mahl</u> uh fie)

a person who dislikes others

> *The Grinch was such a **misanthrope** that even the sight of children singing made him angry.*

Synonym: curmudgeon

. . . .

a written note or letter

> *Priscilla spent hours composing a romantic **missive** for Elvis.*

Synonym: message

. . . .

to calm or make less severe

> *Their argument was so intense that is was difficult to believe any compromise would **mollify** them.*

Synonyms: appease; assuage; conciliate; pacify

Monastic
adj
(muh <u>naas</u> tihk)

· ·

Mores
noun
(<u>mawr</u> ayz)

· ·

Multifarious
adj
(muhl tuh <u>faar</u> ee uhs)

extremely plain or secluded, as in a monastery

*The philosopher retired to his **monastic** lodgings to contemplate life free from any worldly distraction.*

Synonyms: austere; contemplative; disciplined; regimented; self-abnegating

• •

fixed customs or manners; moral attitudes

*In keeping with the **mores** of ancient Roman society, Nero held a celebration every weekend.*

Synonyms: conventions; practices

• •

diverse

*Ken opened the hotel room window, letting in the **multifarious** noises of the great city.*

Synonyms: assorted; indiscriminate; hetergenous; legion; motley; multifold; multiform ; multiplex; multivarious; populous; varied

Nadir
noun
(<u>nay</u> dihr) (<u>nay</u> duhr)

· ·

Neologism
noun
(noo <u>oh</u> luh ji zuhm)

· ·

Nominal
adj
(<u>nah</u> mihn uhl)

lowest point

> *As Joey waited in line to audition for the diaper commercial, he realized he had reached the **nadir** of his acting career.*

Synonyms: bottom; depth; pit

. . . .

new word or expression

> *Aunt Mable simply does not understand today's youth; she is perplexed by their clothing, music, and **neologisms**.*

Synonyms: slang; slip-of-the-tongue

. . . .

existing in name only; negligible

> *A **nominal** but far from devoted member of the high school yearbook committee, she rarely attends meetings.*

Synonyms: minimal; titular

Oblique
adj
(oh <u>bleek</u>)

. . . .

Obsequious
adj
(uhb <u>see</u> kwee uhs)

. . . .

Onerous
adj
(<u>oh</u> neh ruhs)

indirect, evasive; misleading, devious

> *Usually open and friendly, Reinaldo has been behaving in a curiously **oblique** manner lately.*

Synonyms: glancing; slanted; tangential

. . . .

overly submissive and eager to please

> *The **obsequious** new associate made sure to compliment her supervisor's tie and agree with him on every issue.*

Synonyms: compliant; deferential; servile; subservient

. . . .

troublesome and oppressive; burdensome

> *The assignment was so extensive and difficult to manage that it proved **onerous** to the team in charge of it.*

Synonyms: arduous; backbreaking; burdensome; cumbersome; difficult; exacting; formidable; hard; laborious; oppressive; rigorous; taxing; trying

Opine
verb
(oh <u>pien</u>)

• •

Ossify
verb
(<u>ah</u> sih fie)

• •

Ostensible
adj
(ah <u>stehn</u> sih buhl)

to express an opinion

> *At the "Let's Chat Talk Show," the audience member **opined** that the guest was in the wrong.*

Synonyms: point out; voice

. . . .

to change into bone; to become hardened or set in a rigidly conventional pattern

> *The forensics expert ascertained the body's age based on the degree to which the facial structure had **ossified**.*

. . . .

apparent

> *The **ostensible** reason for his visit was to borrow a book, but he secretly wanted to chat with the lovely Wanda.*

Synonyms: represented; supposed; surface

Pallid
adj
(<u>paa</u> lihd)

· ·

Paragon
noun
(<u>par</u> uh gohn)

· ·

Parley
noun
(<u>par</u> lee)

lacking color or liveliness

*The old drugstore's **pallid** window could not compete with Wal-Mart's extravagant display next door.*

Synonyms: ashen; blanched; ghostly; pale; wan

. . . .

model of excellence or perfection

*He is the **paragon** of what a judge should be: honest, intelligent, hardworking, and just.*

Synonyms: apotheosis; ideal; quintessence; standard

. . . .

discussion, usually between enemies

*The **parley** between the rival cheerleading teams resulted in neither side admitting that they copied the other's dance moves.*

Synonyms: debate; dialogue; negotiations; talks

Pathogenic
adj
(paa thoh <u>jehn</u> ihk)

· ·

Peccadillo
noun
(pehk uh <u>dih</u> loh)

· ·

Pedant
noun
(<u>peh</u> daant)

causing disease

*Bina's research on the origins of **pathogenic** microorganisms should help stop the spread of disease.*

Synonyms: infecting; noxious

• •

minor sin or offense

*Gabriel tends to harp on his brother's **peccadillos** and never lets him live them down.*

Synonyms: failing; fault; lapse; misstep

• •

someone who shows off learning

*The graduate instructor's tedious and excessive commentary on the subject soon gained her a reputation as a **pedant**.*

Synonyms: doctrinaire; nit-picker; pedagogue; scholar; schoolmaster; sophist

Penury
noun
(<u>pehn</u> yuh ree)

. . . .

Perspicacious
adj
(puhr spuh <u>kay</u> shuhs)

. . . .

Phlegmatic
adj
(flehg <u>maa</u> tihk)

an oppressive lack of resources (as money); severe poverty

> *Once a famous actor, he eventually died in **penury** and anonymity.*

Synonyms: destitution; impoverishment

• •

shrewd; astute; keen-witted

> *Inspector Poirot used his **perspicacious** mind to solve mysteries.*

Synonyms: insightful; intelligent; sagacious

• •

calm and unemotional in temperament

> *Although the bomb could go off at any moment, the **phlegmatic** demolition expert remained calm and unafraid.*

Synonyms: apathetic; calm; emotionless; impassive; indifferent; passionless; unemotional

Pithy
adj
(<u>pih</u> thee)

• •

Plastic
adj
(<u>plaa</u> stihk)

• •

Plebeian
adj
(plee <u>bee</u> uhn)

concise; succinct; to the point

*Martha's **pithy** comments during the interview must have been impressive because she got the job.*

Synonyms: brief; compact; laconic; terse

. . . .

able to be molded, altered or bent

*The new material was very **plastic** and could be formed into products of vastly different shape.*

Synonyms: adaptable; ductile; malleable; pliant

. . . .

crude or coarse; characteristic of commoners

*After five weeks of rigorous studying, the graduate settled in for a weekend of **plebeian** socializing and television watching.*

Synonyms: conventional; unrefined

Politic
adj
(<u>pah</u> lih tihk)

. . . .

Polyglot
noun
(<u>pah</u> lee glaht)

. . . .

Prattle
noun
(<u>praa</u> tuhl)

shrewd and practical in managing or dealing with things; diplomatic

> *She was wise to curb her tongue and was able to explain her problem to the judge in a respectful and **politic** manner.*

Synonym: tactful

• •

a speaker of many languages

> *Ling's extensive travels have helped her to become a true **polyglot**.*

• •

meaningless, foolish talk

> *Her husband's mindless **prattle** drove Heidi insane; sometimes she wished he would just shut up.*

Synonyms: babble; blather; chatter; drivel; gibberish

Precipitate
verb
(preh <u>sih</u> puh tayt)

· ·

Prescient
adj
(<u>preh</u> shuhnt)

· ·

Probity
noun
(<u>proh</u> bih tee)

to throw violently or bring about abruptly; lacking deliberation

> *Theirs was a **precipitate** marriage–they had only known each other for two weeks before they wed.*

Synonyms: abrupt; hasty; headlong; hurried; ill-considered; impetuous; impulsive; prompt; rash; reckless; sudden

• •

having foresight

> *Jonah's decision to sell the apartment seemed to be a **prescient** one, as its value soon dropped by half.*

Synonyms: augural; divinatory; mantic; oracular; premonitory

• •

complete honesty and integrity

> *George Washington's reputation for **probity** is illustrated in the legend about his inability to lie after he chopped down the cherry tree.*

Synonyms: integrity; morality; rectitude; uprightness; virtue

Propriety
noun
(pruh <u>prie</u> uh tee)

· ·

Puerile
adj
(<u>pyoo</u> ruhl)

· ·

Pugilism
noun
(<u>pyoo</u> juhl ih suhm)

the quality of behaving in a proper manner; obeying rules and customs

> *The aristocracy maintained a high level of **propriety**, adhering to even the most minor social rules.*

Synonyms: appropriateness; decency; decorum; modesty

• •

childish; immature; silly

> *Olivia's boyfriend's **puerile** antics are really annoying; sometimes he acts like a five-year-old!*

Synonyms: infantile; jejune; juvenile

• •

boxing

> ***Pugilism** has been defended as a positive outlet for aggressive impulses.*

Synonyms: fighting; sparring

Quixotic
adj
(kwihk <u>sah</u> tihk)

• •

Raconteur
noun
(raa cahn <u>tuhr</u>)

• •

Redress
noun
(<u>rih</u> drehs)

overly idealistic, impractical

The practical Danuta was skeptical of her roommate's ***quixotic*** *plans to build a roller coaster in their yard.*

Synonyms: capricious; impulsive; romantic; unrealistic

. . . .

witty, skillful storyteller

The ***raconteur*** *kept all the passengers entertained with his stories during the six-hour flight.*

Synonyms: anecdotalist; monologist

. . . .

relief from wrong or injury

Seeking ***redress*** *for the injuries she had received in the accident, Doreen sued the driver of the truck that had hit her.*

Synonyms: amends; indemnity; quittance; reparation; restitution

Rejoinder
noun
(rih <u>joyn</u> duhr)

∙ ∙

Ribald
adj
(<u>rih</u> buhld)

∙ ∙

Sacrosanct
adj
(<u>saa</u> kroh saankt)

response

> *Patrick tried desperately to think of a clever **rejoinder** to Marianna's joke, but he couldn't.*

Synonyms: retort; riposte

. . . .

humorous in a vulgar way

> *The court jester's **ribald** brand of humor delighted the rather uncouth king.*

Synonyms: coarse; gross; indelicate; lewd; obscene

. . . .

extremely sacred; beyond criticism

> *Many people considered Mother Teresa to be **sacrosanct** and would not tolerate any criticism of her.*

Synonyms: holy; inviolable; off-limits

Salient
adj
(<u>say</u> lee uhnt)

· ·

Sanguine
adj
(<u>saan</u> gwuhn)

· ·

Sardonic
adj
(sahr <u>dah</u> nihk)

prominent; of notable significance

*His most **salient** characteristic is his tendency to dominate every conversation.*

Synonyms: marked; noticeable; outstanding

• •

ruddy; cheerfully optimistic

*A **sanguine** person thinks the glass is half full, whereas a depressed person thinks it's half empty.*

Synonyms: confident; hopeful; positive; rosy; rubicund

• •

cynical; scornfully mocking

*Isabella was offended by the **sardonic** way in which her date made fun of her ideas and opinions.*

Synonyms: acerbic; caustic; sarcastic; satirical; snide

Sedition
noun
(sih <u>dih</u> shuhn)

• •

Seraphic
adj
(seh <u>rah</u> fihk)

• •

Soporific
adj
(sahp uhr <u>ihf</u> ihk)

behavior that promotes rebellion or civil disorder against the state

*Li was arrested for **sedition** after he gave a fiery speech in the main square.*

Synonyms: conspiracy; insurrection

. . . .

angelic; sweet

*Selena's **seraphic** appearance belied her nasty, bitter personality.*

Synonyms: cherubic; heavenly

. . . .

causing sleep or lethargy

*The movie proved to be so **soporific** that soon loud snores were heard throughout the cinema.*

Synonyms: hypnotic; narcotic; slumberous; somnolent

Spartan
adj
(<u>spahr</u> tihn)

. . . .

Specious
adj
(<u>spee</u> shuhs)

. . . .

Stentorian
adj
(stehn <u>tohr</u> ee yehn)

highly self-disciplined; frugal; austere

> *When he was in training, the athlete preferred to live in a **spartan** room, so he could shut out all distractions.*

Synonyms: restrained; simple

• •

deceptively attractive; seemingly plausible but fallacious

> *The student's **specious** excuse for being late sounded legitimate, but was proved otherwise when his teacher called his home.*

Synonyms: illusory; ostensible; plausible; sophistic; spurious

• •

extremely loud

> *Cullen couldn't hear her speaking over the **stentorian** din of the game on TV.*

Synonyms: clamorous; noisy

Stolid
adj
(<u>stah</u> lihd)

· ·

Sublime
adj
(suh <u>bliom</u>)

· ·

Surfeit
noun
(<u>suhr</u> fiht)

unemotional; lacking sensitivity

*The prisoner appeared **stolid** and unaffected by the judge's harsh sentence.*

Synonyms: apathetic; impassive; indifferent; phlegmatic; stoical; unconcerned

• •

lofty or grand

*The music was so **sublime** that it transformed the rude surroundings into a special place.*

Synonyms: august; exalted; glorious; grand; magnificent; majestic; noble; resplendent; superb

• •

excessive amount

*Because of the **surfeit** of pigs, pork prices have never been lower.*

Synonyms: glut; plethora; repletion; superfluity; surplus

Sycophant
noun
(<u>sih</u> kuh fuhnt)

• •

Syncopation
noun
(oihn cuh <u>pay</u> shun)

• •

Tacit
adj
(<u>taa</u> siht)

a self-serving flatterer; yes-man

> *Dreading criticism, the actor surrounded himself with admirers and sycophants.*

Synonyms: bootlicker; fawner; lickspittle; toady

. . . .

temporary irregularity in musical rhythm

> *A jazz enthusiast will appreciate the use of syncopation in this musical genre.*

. . . .

done without using words

> *Although not a word was said, everyone in the room knew that a tacit agreement had been made about what course of action to take.*

Synonyms: implicit; implied; undeclared; unsaid; unuttered

Talon
noun
(<u>taa</u> luhn)

. . . .

Toady
noun
(<u>toh</u> dee)

. . . .

Torpor
noun
(<u>tohr</u> puhr)

claw of an animal, especially a bird of prey

> *A vulture holds its prey in its **talons** while it dismembers it with its beak.*

Synonyms: claw; nail

. . . .

one who flatters in the hope of gaining favors

> *The king was surrounded by **toadies** who rushed to agree with whatever outrageous thing he said.*

Synonyms: parasite; sycophant

. . . .

extreme mental and physical sluggishness

> *After surgery, the patient's **torpor** lasted several hours until the anesthesia wore off.*

Synonyms: apathy; languor

Trenchant
adj
(<u>trehn</u> chuhnt)

• •

Turgid
adj
(<u>tuhr</u> jihd)

• •

Tyro
noun
(<u>tie</u> roh)

acute, sharp, incisive; forceful, effective

> *Tyrone's **trenchant** observations in class made him the professor's favorite student.*

Synonyms: biting; caustic; cutting; keen

• •

swollen as from a fluid, bloated

> *In the process of osmosis, water passes through the walls of **turgid** cells, ensuring that they never contain too much water.*

Synonym: distended

• •

beginner, novice

> *An obvious **tyro** at salsa, Millicent received no invitations to dance.*

Synonyms: apprentice; fledgling; greenhorn; neophyte; tenderfoot

Umbrage
noun
(<u>uhm</u> brihj)

• •

Upbraid
verb
(uhp <u>brayd</u>)

• •

Usury
noun
(<u>yoo</u> zhuh ree)

offense; resentment

> *The businessman took **umbrage** at the security guard's accusation that he had shoplifted a packet of gum.*

Synonyms: asperity; dudgeon; ire; pique; rancor

· ·

to scold sharply

> *The teacher **upbraided** the student for scrawling graffiti all over the walls of the school.*

Synonyms: berate; chide; rebuke; reproach; tax

· ·

the practice of lending money at exorbitant rates

> *The moneylender was convicted of **usury** when it was discovered that he charged 50 percent interest on all his loans.*

Synonym: loan-sharking

Variegated
adj
(<u>vaar</u> ee uh <u>gayt</u> ehd)

· ·

Verdant
adj
(<u>vuhr</u> dnt)

· ·

Vex
verb
(vehks)

varied; marked with different colors

> *The **variegated** foliage of the jungle allows it to support thousands of different animal species.*

Synonym: diversified

· ·

green with vegetation; inexperienced

> *He wandered deep into the **verdant** woods in search of mushrooms and other edible flora.*

Synonyms: grassy; leafy; wooded

· ·

to annoy; irritate; puzzle; confuse

> *The old man who loved his peace and quiet was **vexed** by his neighbor's loud music.*

Synonyms: annoy; bother; chafe; exasperate; irk; nettle; peeve; provoke

Viscous
adj
(<u>vih</u> skuhs)

. . . .

Wan
adj
(wahn)

. . . .

Wanton
adj
(<u>wahn</u> tuhn)

thick and adhesive, like a slow-flowing fluid

*Most **viscous** liquids, like oil or honey, become even thicker as they are cooled down.*

Synonyms: gelatinous; glutinous; thick

• •

sickly pale

*The sick child had a **wan** face, in contrast to her rosy-cheeked sister.*

Synonyms: ashen; sickly

• •

undisciplined; unrestrained; reckless

*The townspeople were outraged by the **wanton** display of disrespect when they discovered the statue of the town founder covered in graffiti.*

Synonyms: capricious; lewd; licentious

Winsome
adj
(<u>wihn</u> suhm)

. . . .

Wizened
adj
(<u>wih</u> zuhnd)

. . . .

Xenophobia
noun
(zee nuh <u>foh</u> bee uh)

charming; happily engaging

> *Lenore gave the doorman a **winsome** smile, and he let her pass to the front of the line.*

Synonyms: attractive; delightful

• •

shriveled; withered; wrinkled

> *The **wizened** old man was told that the plastic surgery necessary to make him look young again would cost more money than he could imagine.*

Synonyms: atrophied; desiccated; gnarled; wasted

• •

a fear or hatred of foreigners or strangers

> *Countries in which **xenophobia** is prevalent often have more restrictive immigration policies than countries that are more open to foreign influences.*

Synonyms: bigotry; chauvinism; prejudice

Yoke
verb
(yohk)

• •

Zealot
noun
(<u>zeh</u> luht)

• •

to join together

> *As soon as the farmer had **yoked** his oxen together, he began to plow the fields.*

Synonyms: bind; harness; pair

. . . .

someone passionately devoted to a cause

> *The religious **zealot** had no time for those who failed to share his strong beliefs.*

Synonyms: enthusiast; fanatic; militant; radical

. . . .

Abase
verb
(uh <u>bays</u>)

· ·

Abate
verb
(uh <u>bayt</u>)

· ·

Abdicate
verb
(<u>aab</u> duh kayt)

HARDEST

to humble; to disgrace

*My intention was not to **abase** the comedian.*

Synonyms: demean; humiliate

. . . .

to reduce in amount, degree, or severity

*As the hurricane's force **abated**, the winds dropped and the sea became calm.*

Synonyms: ebb; lapse; let up; moderate; relent; slacken; subside; wane

. . . .

to give up a position, right, or power

*With the angry mob clamoring outside the palace, the king **abdicated** his throne and fled.*

Synonyms: cede; relinquish; resign; quit; yield

Aberrant
adj
(uh <u>ber</u> unt)

• •

Abjure
verb
(aab <u>jur</u>)

• •

Abscond
verb
(aab <u>skahnd</u>)

deviating from what is normal or expected

> *Since he had been a steady, cheerful worker for many years, his fellow postal workers did not expect his **aberrant** burst of rage.*

Synonyms: abnormal; anomalous; deviant; divergent; errant; irregular

• •

to reject; abandon formally

> *The spy **abjured** his allegiance to the United States when he defected to Russia.*

Synonyms: forswear; recall; recant; retract; take back

• •

to leave secretly

> *The patron **absconded** from the restaurant without paying his bill by sneaking out the back door.*

Synonyms: decamp; escape; flee

Abstemious
adj
(aab <u>stee</u> me uhs)

· ·

Acidulous
adj
(uh <u>si</u> juh luhs)

· ·

Alacrity
noun
(uh <u>laak</u> crih tee)

moderate in appetite

> *Because Alyce is a vegetarian, she was only able to eat an **abstemious** meal at the Texas Steakhouse.*

Synonyms: abstinent; continent; self-restraining; sober; temperate

• •

sour in taste or manner

> *The **acidulous** taste of the spoiled milk made the young boy's lips pucker.*

Synonyms: acerbic; acetose; biting; piquant; pungent; tart

• •

speed or quickness

> *The restaurant won a reputation for fine service since the wait staff responded to their clients' requests with **alacrity**.*

Synonyms: celerity; dispatch; haste; swiftness

Amortize
verb
(uh <u>mohr</u> tiez)

. . . .

Anachronism
noun
(uh <u>naak</u> ruh nih suhm)

. . . .

Anodyne
noun
(<u>aah</u> nuh dien)

to diminish by installment payments

> *While college students are notorious for accumulating credit card debt, they are not as well known for **amortizing** it.*

. . . .

something out of place in time

> *The aged hippie used **anachronistic** phrases like "groovy" and "far out" that had not been popular for years.*

Synonyms: archaism; incongruity

. . . .

something that calms or soothes pain

> *The **anodyne** massage helped remove the knots from the lawyer's tense shoulders.*

Synonyms: narcotic; nepenthe; opiate

Antipathy
noun
(aan <u>tih</u> puh thee)

· ·

Approbation
noun
(aa pruh <u>bay</u> shuhn)

· ·

Arrogate
verb
(<u>aa</u> ruh gayt)

extreme dislike

> *The **antipathy** between fans of the rival soccer teams made the game even more electrifying to watch.*

Synonyms: abhorrence; animosity; animus; antagonism; aversion; dislike; enmity; hatred; hostility; loathing; repellence; repugnance; repulsion; revulsion

• •

approval and praise

> *The **approbation** that Jerry Lewis received in France included a medal from the Ministry of Culture.*

Synonyms: acclaim; adulation; applause; commendation; compliments; exalt; extol; hail; kudos; praise

• •

to claim without justification; to claim for oneself without right

> *Gretchen watched in astonishment as her boss **arrogated** the credit for her brilliant work on the project.*

Synonyms: appropriate; presume; take

Assuage
verb
(uh <u>swayj</u>) (uh <u>swayzh</u>) (uh <u>swahzh</u>)

• •

Augury
noun
(<u>aw</u> gyuh ree) (<u>aw</u> guh ree)

• •

Bilk
verb
(bihlk)

to make something unpleasant less severe

> *Like many people, Philip Larkin used alcohol to **assuage** his sense of meaninglessness and despair.*

Synonyms: allay; alleviate; appease; comfort; conciliate; ease; lighten; mitigate; mollify; pacify; palliate; placate; propitiate; relieve; soothe; sweeten

• •

prophecy; prediction of events

> *Troy hoped the rainbow was an **augury** of good things to come.*

Synonyms: auspices; harbinger; omen; portent; presage

• •

to cheat; to defraud

> *When the greedy salesman realized that his customer spoke poor French, he **bilked** the tourist out of 20 euros.*

Synonyms: beat; defraud; diddle; gyp; overreach

Bonhomie
noun
(bah nuh <u>mee</u>)

• •

Burgeon
verb
(<u>buhr</u> juhn)

• •

Calumny
noun
(<u>kaa</u> luhm nee)

good-natured geniality; atmosphere of good cheer

*The aspects of her job that Dana loved the most were the flexible hours and the pleasant **bonhomie** in the office*

. . . .

to grow and flourish

*Faulkner neither confirmed nor denied stories about himself, allowing rumor to **burgeon** where it would.*

Synonyms: bloom; burgeon; flourish; prosper; thrive

. . . .

a false and malicious accusation; misrepresentation

*The unscrupulous politician used **calumny** to bring down his opponent in the senatorial race.*

Synonyms: defamation; libel; slander

Canard
noun
(kuh <u>nard</u>)

. . . .

Capricious
adj
(kuh <u>prce</u> shul is) (kuh <u>prih</u> shuhs)

. . . .

Catholic
adj
(<u>kaa</u> thuh lihk) (<u>kaa</u> thlihk)

a lie

> *That tabloid's feature story about a goat giving birth to a human child was clearly a **canard**.*

Synonyms: falsehood; falsity; fib; misrepresentation; prevarication; tale; untruth

• •

changing one's mind quickly and often

> *Queen Elizabeth I was quite **capricious**; her courtiers could never be sure which one would catch her fancy.*

Synonyms: arbitrary; chance; changeable; erratic; fickle; inconstant; mercurial; random; whimsical; willful

• •

universal; broad and comprehensive

> *Hot tea with honey is a **catholic** remedy for a sore throat.*

Synonyms: extensive; general

Chicanery
noun
(shih <u>kayn</u> ree) (shi <u>kay</u> nuh ree)

· ·

Circumspect
adj
(<u>suhr</u> kuhm spehkt)

· ·

Cogent
adj
(<u>koh</u> juhnt)

deception by means of craft or guile

*Dishonest used-car salesmen often use **chicanery** to sell their beat-up old cars.*

Synonyms: artifice; conniving; craftiness; deception; deviousness; misrepresentation; pettifoggery; shadiness; sneakiness; sophistry; subterfuge; underhandedness

• •

cautious; aware of potential consequences

*She was very **circumspect** in her language and behavior when first introduced to her fiancee's parents.*

Synonyms: alert; cautious; heedful; mindful; prudent; solicitous; vigilant; wary

• •

convincing and well-reasoned

*Swayed by the **cogent** argument of the defense, the jury had no choice but to acquit the defendant.*

Synonyms: convincing; persuasive; solid; sound; telling; valid

Contumacious
adj
(kahn tuh <u>may</u> shuhs)

• •

Corroborate
verb
(kuh <u>rahb</u> uhr ayt)

• •

Cosset
verb
(<u>kah</u> suht)

rebellious

> *The **contumacious** teenager ran away from home when her parents told her she was grounded.*

Synonyms: factious; insubordinate; insurgent; mutinous; rebellious; seditious

• •

to support with evidence

> *All the DA needed were fingerprints to **corroborate** the witness's testimony that he saw the defendant in the victim's apartment.*

Synonyms: authenticate; back; buttress; confirm; substantiate; validate; verify

• •

to pamper, treat with great care

> *Marta just loves to **cosset** her first and only grandchild.*

Synonyms: cater to; cuddle; dandle; fondle; love; pamper; pet; spoil

Coterie
noun
(<u>koh</u> tuh ree) (koh tuh <u>ree</u>)

. . . .

Cupidity
noun
(kyoo <u>pih</u> dih tee)

. . . .

Declivity
noun
(dih <u>klih</u> vih tee)

an intimate group of persons with a similar purpose

*Angel invited a **coterie** of fellow stamp enthusiasts to a stamp-trading party.*

Synonyms: clique; set

· ·

greed; strong desire

*The thief stared at the shining jewels with **cupidity** in his gleaming eyes.*

Synonyms: avarice; covetousness; rapacity

· ·

downward slope

*Because the village was situated on the **declivity** of a hill, it never flooded.*

Synonyms: decline; descent; grade; slant; tilt

Deleterious
adj
(dehl ih <u>teer</u> ee uhs)

. . . .

Desultory
adj
(dehs <u>uhl</u> tohr ee) (<u>dehz</u> uhl tohr ee)

. . . .

Diaphonous
adj
(die <u>aaf</u> uh nuhs)

subtly or unexpectedly harmful

> *If only we had known the clocks were defective before putting them on the market, it wouldn't have been quite so **deleterious** to our reputation.*

Synonyms: adverse; inimical; injurious; hurtful

• •

jumping from one thing to another; disconnected

> *Athena had a **desultory** academic record; she had changed majors 12 times in 3 years.*

Synonyms: aimless; disconnected; erratic; haphazard; indiscriminate; objectless; purposeless; random; stray; unconsidered; unplanned

• •

allowing light to show through; delicate

> *These **diaphanous** curtains do nothing to block out the sunlight.*

Synonyms: gauzy; sheer; tenuous; translucent; transparent

Diffident
adj
(<u>dih</u> fih dint)

• •

Dilatory
adj
(<u>dihl</u> uh tohr ee)

• •

Disabuse
verb
(dih suh <u>byuze</u>)

lacking self-confidence

*Steve's **diffidence** during the job interview stemmed from his nervous nature and lack of experience in the field.*

Synonyms: backward; bashful; coy; demure; modest; retiring; self-effacing; shy; timid

• •

intended to delay

*The congressman used **dilatory** measures to delay the passage of the bill.*

Synonyms: dragging; flagging; laggard; lagging; slow; slow-footed; slow-going; slow-paced; tardy

• •

set right; free from error

*Galileo's observations **disabused** scholars of the notion that the Sun revolved around the Earth.*

Synonyms: correct; undeceive

Distaff
noun
(<u>dis</u> taf)

· ·

Diurnal
adj
(die <u>uhr</u> nuhl)

· ·

Divine
verb
(dih <u>vien</u>)

the female branch of a family

> *The lazy husband refused to cook dinner for his wife, joking that the duty belongs to the **distaff's** side.*

. . . .

existing during the day

> ***Diurnal** creatures tend to become inactive during the night.*

Synonyms: daylight; daytime

. . . .

to foretell or know by inspiration

> *The fortune-teller **divined** from the pattern of the tea leaves that her customer would marry five times.*

Synonyms: auger; foresee; intuit; predict; presage

Dyspeptic
adj
(dihs <u>pehp</u> tihk)

. . . .

Edify
verb
(<u>eh</u> duh fie)

. . . .

Effrontery
noun
(ih <u>fruhnt</u> uhr ee) (eh <u>fruhnt</u> uhr ee)

suffering from indigestion; gloomy and irritable

*The **dyspeptic** young man cast a gloom over the party the minute he walked in.*

Synonyms: acerb; melancholy; morose; solemn; sour

. . . .

to instruct morally and spiritually

*The guru was paid to **edify** the actress in the ways of Buddhism.*

Synonyms: educate; enlighten; guide; teach

. . . .

impudent boldness; audacity

*The receptionist had the **effrontery** to laugh out loud when the CEO tripped over a computer wire and fell flat on his face.*

Synonyms: brashness; gall; nerve; presumption; temerity

Encomium
noun
(ehn <u>koh</u> me uhm)

. . . .

Enervate
verb
(ehn <u>uhr</u> vayt)

. . . .

Enumerate
verb
(ih <u>noo</u> muhr ayt)

warm praise

> *Georgias's **"Encomium** to Helen" was written as a tribute to Helen of Troy.*

Synonyms: citation; eulogy; panegyric; salutation; tribute

• •

to reduce in strength

> *The guerrillas hoped that a series of surprise attacks would **enervate** the regular army.*

Synonyms: debilitate; enfeeble; sap; weaken

• •

to count, list, or itemize

> *Before making his decision, Jacob asked the waiter to **enumerate** the different varieties of ice cream that the restaurant carried.*

Synonyms: catalog; index; tabulate

Epicure
noun
(eh pih <u>kyoor</u>) (<u>eh</u> pih kyuhr)

. . . .

Equivocate
verb
(ih <u>kwihv</u> uh kayt)

. . . .

Ersatz
adj
(<u>uhr</u> sats) (uhr <u>sats</u>)

person with refined taste in food and wine

> *Niren is an **epicure** who always throws the most splendid dinner parties.*

Synonyms: bon vivant; connoisseur; gastronome; gastronomer; gastronomist; gourmand; gourmet

• •

to use expressions of double meaning in order to mislead

> *When faced with criticism of his policies, the politician **equivocated** and left all parties thinking he agreed with them.*

Synonyms: ambiguous; evasive; waffling

• •

fake

> *Edda, a fashion maven, knew instantly that her friend's new Kate Spade bag was really an **ersatz** version purchased on the street.*

Synonyms: artificial; dummy; false; imitation; mock; sham; simulated; spurious; substitute

Eschew
verb
(ehs <u>choo</u>)

. . . .

Estimable
adj
(<u>eh</u> stuh muh buhl)

. . . .

Euphony
noun
(<u>yoo</u> fuh nee)

to shun; to avoid (as something wrong or distasteful)

*The filmmaker **eschewed** artificial light for her actors, resulting in a stark movie style.*

Synonyms: avoid; bilk; elude; escape; evade; shun; shy

• •

admirable

*Most people consider it **estimable** that Mother Teresa spent her life helping the poor of India.*

Synonyms: admirable; commendable; creditable; honorable; laudable; meritorious; praiseworthy; respectable; venerable; worthy

• •

pleasant, harmonious sound

*To their loving parents, the children's orchestra performance sounded like **euphony**, although an outside observer probably would have called it a cacophony of hideous sounds.*

Synonyms: harmony; melody; music; sweetness

Exacerbate
verb
(ihg <u>zaas</u> uhr bayt)

. . . .

Exculpate
verb
(<u>ehk</u> skuhl payt) (<u>ihk</u> skuhl payt)

. . . .

Exigent
adj
(<u>ehk</u> suh juhnt)

to make worse

> *It is unwise to take aspirin to try to relieve heartburn since instead of providing relief it will only **exacerbate** the problem.*

Synonyms: aggravate; annoy; intensify; irritate; provoke

. . . .

to clear from blame; prove innocent

> *The legal system is intended to convict those who are guilty and **exculpate** those who are innocent.*

Synonyms: absolve; acquit; clear; exonerate; vindicate

. . . .

urgent; requiring immediate action

> *The patient was losing blood so rapidly that it was **exigent** to stop the source of the bleeding.*

Synonyms: critical; imperative; needed; urgent

Exonerate
verb
(ihg <u>zahn</u> uh rayt)

• •

Exponent
noun
(ihk <u>spoh</u> nuhnt) (<u>ehk</u> spoh nuhnt)

• •

Expurgate
verb
(<u>ehk</u> spuhr gayt)

to clear of blame

> *The fugitive was **exonerated** when another criminal confessed to committing the crime.*

Synonyms: absolve; acquit; clear; exculpate; vindicate

. . . .

one who champions or advocates

> *The vice president was an enthusiastic **exponent** of computer technology.*

Synonyms: representative; supporter

. . . .

to censor

> *Government propagandists **expurgated** all negative references to the dictator from the film.*

Synonyms: bowdlerize; cut; sanitize

Fatuous
adj
(<u>fah</u> choo uhs)

• •

Fawn
verb
(fahn)

• •

Fervid
adj
(<u>fuhr</u> vihd)

stupid; foolishly self-satisfied

> *Ted's **fatuous** comments always embarrassed his keen-witted wife at parties.*

Synonyms: absurd; ludicrous; preposterous; ridiculous; silly

• •

to grovel

> *The understudy **fawned** over the director in hopes of being cast in the part on a permanent basis.*

Synonyms: bootlick; grovel; pander; toady

• •

intensely emotional, feverish

> *The fans of Maria Callas were particularly **fervid**, doing anything to catch a glimpse of the great opera singer.*

Synonyms: burning; impassioned; passionate; vehement; zealous

Foment
verb
(foh <u>mehnt</u>)

· ·

Ford
verb
(fohrd)

· ·

Fractious
adj
(<u>fraak</u> shuhs)

to arouse or incite

*The rebels tried to **foment** revolution through their attacks on the government.*

Synonyms: agitate; impassion; inflame; instigate; kindle

. . . .

to cross a body of water by wading

*Because of the recent torrential rains, the cowboys were unable to **ford** the swollen river.*

Synonyms: traverse; wade

. . . .

unruly; rebellious

*The general had a hard time maintaining discipline among his **fractious** troops.*

Synonyms: contentious; cranky; peevish; quarrelsome

Furtive
adj
(<u>fuhr</u> tihv)

• •

Gambol
verb
(<u>gaam</u> buhl)

• •

Glib
adj
(glihb)

secret; stealthy

> *Glenn was **furtive** when he peered out of the corner of his eye at the stunningly beautiful model.*

Synonyms: clandestine; covert; shifty; surreptitious; underhand

· ·

to dance or skip around playfully

> *From her office, Amy enviously watched the playful puppies **gambol** around Central Park.*

Synonyms: caper; cavort; frisk; frolic; rollick; romp

· ·

fluent in an insincere manner; offhand; casual

> *The slimy politician managed to continue gaining supporters because he was a **glib** speaker.*

Synonyms: easy; superficial

Hapless
adj
(<u>haap</u> luhs)

· ·

Husband
verb
(<u>huhz</u> buhnd)

· ·

Ignoble
adj
(ihg <u>noh</u> buhl)

unfortunate; having bad luck

> *I wish someone would give that poor, **hapless** soul some food and shelter.*

Synonyms: ill-fated; ill-starred; jinxed; luckless; unlucky

• •

to manage economically; to use sparingly

> *The cyclist paced herself at the start of the race, knowing that if she **husbanded** her resources she'd have the strength to break out of the pack later on.*

Synonym: conserve

• •

having low moral standards, not noble in character; mean

> *The photographer was paid a princely sum for the picture of the self-proclaimed ethicist in the **ignoble** act of pick-pocketing.*

Synonyms: lowly; vulgar

Impecunious
adj
(ihm pih <u>kyoo</u> nyuhs) (ihm pih <u>kyoo</u> nee uhs)

• •

Imperturbable
adj
(im puhr <u>tuhr</u> buh buhl)

• •

Impious
adj
(<u>ihm</u> pee uhs) (ihm <u>pie</u> uhs)

poor; having no money

> *After the stock market crashed, many former million-aires found themselves **impecunious**.*

Synonyms: destitute; impoverished; indigent; needy; penniless

• •

not capable of being disturbed

> *The counselor had so much experience dealing with distraught children that she was **imperturbable**, even when faced with the wildest tantrums.*

Synonyms: composed; dispassionate; impassive; serene; stoical

• •

not devout in religion

> *The nun cut herself off from her **impious** family after she entered the convent.*

Synonyms: immoral; irreverent; profane

Imprecation
noun
(ihm prih <u>kay</u> shuhn)

• •

Impugn
verb
(ihm <u>pyoon</u>)

• •

Incarnadine
adj
(in <u>car</u> nuh deen)

a curse

*Spouting violent **imprecations**, Hank searched for the person who had vandalized his truck.*

Synonym: damnation

• •

to call into question; to attack verbally

*"How dare you **impugn** my motives?" protested the lawyer, on being accused of ambulance chasing.*

Synonyms: challenge; dispute

• •

blood-red in color

*At his mother's mention of his baby pictures, the shy boy's cheeks turned **incarnadine** with embarrassment.*

Synonyms: reddened; ruby; ruddy

Inchoate
adj
(ihn <u>koh</u> uht)

. . . .

Inculcate
verb
(ihn <u>kuhl</u> kayt) (<u>ihn</u> kuhl kayt)

. . . .

Indolent
adj
(<u>ihn</u> duh luhnt)

not fully formed; disorganized

> *The ideas expressed in Nietzsche's mature work also appear in an **inchoate** form in his earliest writing.*

Synonyms: amorphous; incoherent; incomplete; unorganized

• •

to teach; to impress in the mind

> *Most parents **inculcate** their children with their beliefs and ideas instead of allowing their children to develop their own values.*

Synonyms: implant; indoctrinate; instill; preach

• •

habitually lazy; idle

> *Her **indolent** ways got her fired from many jobs.*

Synonyms: fainéant; languid; lethargic; slothful; sluggish

Inimical
adj
(ih <u>nihm</u> ih kuhl)

. . . .

Iniquity
noun
(ih <u>nihk</u> wih tee)

. . . .

Insipid
adj
(in <u>sih</u> pid)

hostile; unfriendly

> *Even though a cease-fire had been in place for months, the two sides were still **inimical** to each other.*

Synonyms: adverse; antagonistic; dissident; recalcitrant

• •

sin; evil act

> *"I promise to close every den of **iniquity** in this town!" thundered the conservative new mayor.*

Synonyms: enormity; immorality; injustice; vice; wickedness

• •

lacking interest or flavor

> *The critic claimed that the painting was **insipid**, containing no interesting qualities at all.*

Synonyms: banal; bland; dull; stale; vapid

Interregnum
noun
(in tuh <u>reg</u> nuhm)

• •

Inure
verb
(ih <u>nyoor</u>)

• •

Investiture
noun
(in <u>ves</u> tuh chur)

interval between reigns

> *When John F. Kennedy was shot, there was a brief **inter-regnum** before Lyndon B. Johnson became president.*

• •

to harden; accustom; become used to

> *Eventually, Hassad became **inured** to the sirens that went off every night and could sleep through them.*

Synonyms: condition; familiarize; habituate

• •

ceremony conferring authority

> *At Napoleon's **investiture**, he grabbed the crown from the Pope's hands and placed it on his head himself.*

Synonyms: inaugural; inauguration; induction; initiation; installation

Invidious
adj
(ihn <u>vihd</u> ee uhs)

• •

Jingoism
noun
(<u>jing</u> goh ihz uhm)

• •

Jocular
adj
(<u>jahk</u> yuh luhr)

envious; obnoxious; offensive; likely to promote ill-will

> *It is cruel and **invidious** for parents to play favorites with their children.*

Synonyms: discriminatory; insulting; jaundiced; resentful

• •

belligerent support of one's country

> *The proffessor's **jingoism** made it difficult for the students to participate in an open political discussion.*

Synonyms: chauvinism; nationalism

• •

playful; humorous

> *The **jocular** old man entertained his grandchildren for hours.*

Synonyms: amusing; comical

Juncture
noun
(<u>juhnk</u> chuhr)

• •

Kudos
noun
(<u>koo</u> dohz)

• •

Lachrymose
adj
(<u>laak</u> ruh mohs)

point of time, especially where two things are joined

*At this **juncture**, I think it would be a good idea for us to take a coffee break.*

Synonyms: confluence; convergence; crisis; crossroads; moment

. . . .

fame, glory, honor

*The actress happily accepted **kudos** from the press for her stunning performance in the film.*

Synonyms: acclaim; accolade; encomium; homage; praise

. . . .

tearful

*Marcella always became **lachrymose** when it was time to bid her daughter good-bye.*

Synonyms: teary; weeping

Lapidary
adj
(<u>laa</u> puh der ee)

· ·

Largess
noun
(laar <u>jehs</u>)

· ·

Laud
verb
(lawd)

relating to precious stones or the art of cutting them

> *Most **lapidary** work today is done with the use of motorized equipment.*

• •

generous giving (as of money) to others who may seem inferior

> *She'd always relied on her parent's **largess**, but after graduation she had to get a job.*

Synonyms: benevolence; boon; compliment; favor; present

• •

to give praise; to glorify

> *Parades and fireworks were staged to **laud** the success of the rebels.*

Synonyms: acclaim; applaud; commend; compliment; exalt; extol; hail; praise

Legerdemain
noun
(lehj uhr duh <u>mayn</u>)

• •

Licentious
adj
(lie <u>sehn</u> shuhs)

• •

Limpid
adj
(<u>lim</u> pihd)

trickery

> *The little boy thought his **legerdemain** was working on his mother, but she in fact knew about every hidden toy and stolen cookie.*

Synonyms: chicanery; conjuring

• •

immoral; unrestrained by society

> *Religious citizens were outraged by the **licentious** exploits of the free-spirited artists living in town.*

Synonyms: lewd; wanton

• •

clear; transparent

> *Fernando could see all the way to the bottom through the pond's **limpid** water.*

Synonyms: lucid; pellucid; serene

Lissome
adj
(<u>lihs</u> uhm)

• •

Lugubrious
adj
(loo <u>goo</u> bree uhs)

• •

Magnate
noun
(<u>maag</u> nayt) (<u>maag</u> niht)

easily flexed; limber; agile

> *The **lissome** yoga instructor twisted herself into shapes that her students could only dream of.*

Synonyms: graceful; lithe; supple

. . . .

sorrowful; mournful; dismal

> *Irish wakes are a rousing departure from the **lugubrious** funeral services to which most people are accustomed.*

Synonyms: funereal; gloomy; melancholy; somber; woeful

. . . .

powerful or influential person

> *The entertainment **magnate** bought two cable TV stations to add to his collection of magazines and publishing houses.*

Synonyms: dignitary; luminary; nabob; potentate; tycoon

Malediction
noun
(maal ih <u>dihk</u> shun)

. . . .

Martinet
noun
(mahr tihn <u>eht</u>)

. . . .

Mendacious
adj
(mehn <u>day</u> shuhs)

a curse; a wish of evil upon another

> *The frog prince looked for a princess to kiss him and put an end to the witch's **malediction**.*

Synonyms: anathema; imprecation

• •

strict disciplinarian; one who rigidly follows rules

> *A complete **martinet**, the official insisted that Pete fill out all the forms again even though he was already familiar with his case.*

Synonyms: dictator; stickler; tyrant

• •

dishonest

> *So many of her stories were **mendacious** that I decided she must be a pathological liar.*

Synonyms: deceitful; false; lying; untruthful

Mendicant
noun
(<u>mehn</u> dih kuhnt)

• •

Mercurial
adj
(muhr <u>kyoor</u> ee uhl)

• •

Meretricious
adj
(mehr ih <u>trihsh</u> uhs)

beggar

"Please, sir, can you spare a dime?" begged the mendicant as the businessman walked past.

Synonyms: panhandler; pauper

• •

quick; shrewd; unpredictable

Her mercurial personality made it difficult to guess how she would react to the bad news.

Synonyms: clever; crafty; volatile; whimsical

• •

gaudy; falsely attractive

The casino's meretricious decor horrified the cultivated interior designer.

Synonyms: flashy; insincere; loud; specious; tawdry

Metaphor
noun
(<u>meht</u> uh fohr) (<u>meht</u> uh fuhr)

• •

Mirth
noun
(muhrth)

• •

Mitigate
verb
(<u>miht</u> ih gayt)

figure of speech comparing two different things

*The **metaphor** "a sea of troubles" suggests a lot of troubles by comparing their number to the vastness of the sea.*

Synonyms: allegory; analogy; simile; symbol

. . . .

frivolity; gaiety; laughter

*Vera's hilarious jokes contributed to the general **mirth** at the dinner party.*

Synonyms: glee; hilarity; jollity; merriment

. . . .

to soften; to lessen

*A judge may **mitigate** a sentence if she decides that a person committed a crime out of need.*

Synonyms: allay; alleviate; assuage; ease; lighten; moderate; mollify; palliate; temper

Molt
verb
(muhlt)

• •

Myopic
adj
(mie <u>ahp</u> ihk) (mie <u>oh</u> pihk)

• •

Neophyte
noun
(<u>nee</u> oh fiet)

to shed hair, skin, or an outer layer periodically

> *The snake **molted** its skin and left it behind in a crumpled mass.*

Synonyms: cast; defoliate; desquamate

• •

lacking foresight; having a narrow view or long-range perspective

> *Not wanting to spend a lot of money up front, the **myopic** business owner would likely suffer the consequences later.*

Synonyms: short-sighted; unthinking

• •

novice; beginner

> *A relative **neophyte** at bowling, Rodolfo rolled all of his balls into the gutter.*

Synonyms: apprentice; greenhorn; tyro

Nettle
verb
(<u>neh</u> tuhl)

• •

Noisome
adj
(<u>noy</u> suhm)

• •

Numismatics
noun
(nu miz <u>maa</u> tiks)

to irritate

> *I don't particularly like having blue hair—I just do it to* **nettle** *my parents.*

Synonyms: annoy; vex

• •

stinking; putrid

> *A dead mouse trapped in your walls produces a* **noisome** *odor.*

Synonyms: disgusting; foul; malodorous

• •

coin collecting

> *Tomas' passion for* **numismatics** *has resulted in an impressive collection of coins from all over the world.*

Obdurate
adj
(<u>ahb</u> duhr uht)

. . . .

Obviate
verb
(<u>ahb</u> vee ayt)

. . . .

Occlude
verb
(uh <u>klood</u>)

hardened in feeling; resistant to persuasion

> *The president was completely **obdurate** on the issue, and no amount of persuasion would change his mind.*

Synonyms: inflexible; intransigent; recalcitrant; tenacious; unyielding

. . . .

to prevent; to make unnecessary

> *The river was shallow enough to wade across at many points, which **obviated** the need for a bridge.*

Synonyms: forestall; preclude; prohibit

. . . .

to stop up; to prevent the passage of

> *A shadow is thrown across the Earth's surface during a solar eclipse, when the light from the sun is **occluded** by the moon.*

Synonyms: barricade; block; close; obstruct

Officious
adj
(uh <u>fihsh</u> uhs)

• •

Opprobrium
noun
(uh <u>pro</u> bree uhm)

• •

Orotund
adj
(<u>or</u> uh tuhnd) (<u>ah</u> ruh tuhnd)

too helpful; meddlesome

> *While planning her wedding, Maya discovered just how* ***officious*** *her future mother-in-law could be.*

Synonyms: eager; unwanted; intrusive

. . . .

public disgrace

> *After the scheme to embezzle the elderly was made public, the treasurer resigned in utter* ***opprobrium***.

Synonyms: discredit; disgrace; dishonor; disrepute; ignominy; infamy; obloquy; shame

. . . .

pompous

> *Roberto soon grew tired of his date's* ***orotund*** *babble about her new job, and decided their first date would probably be their last.*

Synonyms: aureate; bombastic; declamatory; euphuistic; flowery; grandiloquent; magniloquent; oratorical; overblown; sonorous

Ostentation
noun
(ah stehn <u>tay</u> shuhn)

· ·

Palliate
verb
(<u>paa</u> lee ayt)

· ·

Panegyric
noun
(paan uh <u>jeer</u> ihk)

excessive showiness

> The **ostentation** of the Sun King's court is evident in the lavish decoration and luxuriousness of his palace at Versailles.

Synonyms: conspicuousness; flashiness; pretentiousness; showiness

• •

to make less serious; ease

> The alleged crime was so vicious that the defense lawyer could not **palliate** it for the jury.

Synonyms: alleviate; assuage; extenuate; mitigate

• •

elaborate praise; formal hymn of praise

> The director's **panegyric** for the donor who kept his charity going was heart-warming.

Synonyms: compliment; homage

Panoply
noun
(<u>paa</u> nuh plee)

· ·

Pare
verb
(payr)

· ·

Parry
verb
(<u>paar</u> ree)

impressive array

> *Her résumé indicates a **panoply** of skills and accomplishments.*

Synonyms: array; display; fanfare; parade; pomp; shine; show

• •

to trim off excess; reduce

> *The cook's hands were sore after she **pared** hundreds of potatoes for the banquet.*

Synonyms: clip; peel

• •

to ward off or deflect, especially by a quick-witted answer

> *Kari **parried** every question the army officers fired at her, much to their frustration.*

Synonyms: avoid; evade; repel

Pastiche
noun
(pah <u>steesh</u>)

. . . .

Peregrinate
verb
(<u>peh</u> ruh gruh nayt)

. . . .

Perfidious
adj
(puhr <u>fih</u> dee uhs)

piece of literature or music imitating other works

> *The playwright's clever **pastiche** of the well-known children's story had the audience rolling in the aisles.*

Synonyms: medley; spoof

. . . .

to wander from place to place; to travel, especially on foot

> *Shivani enjoyed **peregrinating** the expansive grounds of Central Park.*

Synonyms: journey; traverse; trek

. . . .

willing to betray one's trust

> *The actress's **perfidious** companion revealed all of her intimate secrets to the gossip columnist.*

Synonyms: disloyal; faithless; traitorous; treacherous

Perfunctory
adj
(pur <u>fuhnk</u> tuhr ee)

∙ ∙

Peripatetic
adj
(peh ruh puh <u>teh</u> tihk)

∙ ∙

Potentate
noun
(<u>poh</u> tehn tayt)

done in a routine way; indifferent

> *The machine-like teller processed the transaction and gave the waiting customer a **perfunctory** smile.*

Synonyms: apathetic; automatic; mechanical

• •

wandering from place to place, especially on foot

> *Eleana's **peripatetic** meanderings took her all over the countryside in the summer months.*

Synonyms: itinerant; nomadic; wayfaring

• •

a monarch or ruler with great power

> *Alex was much kinder before he assumed the role of **potentate**.*

Synonyms: dominator; leader

Précis
noun
(<u>pray</u> see) (pray <u>see</u>)

· ·

Prevaricate
verb
(prih <u>vaar</u> uh cayt)

· ·

Proclivity
noun
(proh <u>clih</u> vuh tee)

short summary of facts

*Fara wrote a **précis** of her thesis on the epic poem to share with the class.*

Synonym: summary

. . . .

to lie or deviate from the truth

*Rather than admit that he had overslept again, the employee **prevaricated** and claimed that heavy traffic had prevented him from arriving at work on time.*

Synonyms: equivocate; lie; perjure

. . . .

a natural inclination or predisposition

*Her childhood love of acting, singing, and adoration indicated a **proclivity** for the theater in later life.*

Synonyms: bias; leaning; partiality; penchant; predilection; predisposition; prejudice; propensity

Profligate
adj
(<u>praa</u> flih guht)

· ·

Propitiate
verb
(proh <u>pih</u> shee ayt)

· ·

Pulchritude
noun
(<u>puhl</u> kruh tood)

corrupt; degenerate

Some historians claim that it was the Romans' decadent, **profligate** *behavior that led to the decline of the Roman Empire.*

Synonyms: dissolute; extravagant; improvident; prodigal; wasteful

• •

to conciliate, to appease

Because their gods were angry and vengeful, the Vikings **propitiated** *them with many sacrifices.*

Synonyms: appease; conciliate; mollify; pacify; placate

• •

beauty

The mortals gazed in admiration at Venus, stunned by her incredible **pulchritude**.

Synonyms: comeliness; gorgeousness; handsomeness; loveliness; prettiness

Pusillanimous
adj
(pyoo suh <u>laa</u> nih muhs)

. . . .

Querulous
adj
(<u>kwehr</u> yoo luhs)

. . . .

Quiescent
adj
(kwie <u>eh</u> sihnt)

cowardly; without courage

> *The **pusillanimous** man would not enter the yard where the miniature poodle was barking.*

Synonyms: cowardly; timid

· ·

inclined to complain; irritable

> *Curtis's complaint letter received prompt attention after the company labeled him a **querulous** potential trouble-maker.*

Synonyms: argumentative; cantankerous; petulant; irritable

· ·

motionless

> *Many animals are **quiescent** over the winter months, minimizing activity in order to conserve energy.*

Synonyms: dormant; latent

Rarefy
verb
(<u>rayr</u> uh fie)

• •

Replete
adj
(rih <u>pleet</u>)

• •

Requite
verb
(rih <u>kwiet</u>)

to make thinner or sparser

> *Since the atmosphere **rarefies** as altitudes increase, the air at the top of very tall mountains is too thin to breathe.*

Synonyms: attenuate; thin

• •

abundantly supplied; complete

> *The gigantic supermarket was **replete** with consumer products of every kind.*

Synonyms: abounding; full

• •

to return or repay

> *Thanks for offering to lend me $1,000, but I know I'll never be able to **requite** your generosity.*

Synonyms: compensate; reciprocate

Restive
adj
(<u>reh</u> stihv)

• •

Reticent
adj
(<u>reh</u> tih suhnt)

• •

Rococo
adj
(ruh <u>koh</u> koh) (roh kuh <u>koh</u>)

impatient; uneasy; restless

> *The passengers became **restive** after having to wait in line for hours and began to shout complaints at the airline staff.*

Synonyms: agitated; anxious; fretful

• •

silent; reserved

> *Physically small and verbally **reticent**, Joan Didion often went unnoticed by those she was reporting upon.*

Synonyms: cool; introverted; laconic; standoffish; taciturn; undemonstrative

• •

very highly ornamented; relating to an 18th century artistic style of elaborate ornamentation

> *The ornate furniture in the house reminded Tatiana of the **rococo** style.*

Synonyms: intricate; ornate

Sagacious
adj
(suh <u>gay</u> shuhs)

• •

Salubrious
adj
(suh <u>loo</u> bree uhs)

• •

Satiate
verb
(<u>say</u> shee ayt)

shrewd; wise

*Owls have a reputation for being **sagacious**, perhaps because of their big eyes, which resemble glasses.*

Synonyms: astute; judicious; perspicacious; sage; wise

. . . .

healthful

*Rundown and sickly, Rita hoped that the fresh mountain air would have a **salubrious** effect on her health.*

Synonyms: bracing; curative; medicinal; therapeutic; tonic

. . . .

to satisfy fully or overindulge

*His desire for power was so great that nothing less than complete control of the country could **satiate** it.*

Synonyms: cloy; glut; gorge; surfeit

Scintilla
noun
(sihn <u>tihl</u> uh)

. . . .

Sinecure
noun
(<u>sien</u> ih kyoor)

. . . .

Sobriquet
noun
(<u>soh</u> brih keht)

trace amount

> *This poison is so powerful that no more than a **scintilla** of it is needed to kill a horse.*

Synonyms: atom; iota; mote; spark; speck

• •

a well-paying job or office that requires little or no work

> *The corrupt mayor made sure to set up all his relatives in **sinecures** within the administration.*

• •

nickname

> *One of Ronald Reagan's **sobriquets** was "The Gipper."*

Synonyms: alias; pseudonym

Solecism
noun
(<u>sah</u> lih sishz uhm)

. . . .

Sybarite
noun
(<u>sih</u> buh riet)

. . . .

Taciturn
adj
(<u>taa</u> sih tuhrn)

grammatical mistake; blunder in speech

> *"I ain't going with you," she said, obviously unaware of her* **solecism**.

Synonyms: blooper; faux pas; vulgarism

• •

a person devoted to pleasure and luxury

> *A confirmed* **sybarite**, *the nobleman fainted at the thought of having to leave his palace and live in a small cottage.*

Synonyms: hedonist; pleasuremonger; sensualist

• •

silent; not talkative

> *The clerk's* **taciturn** *nature earned him the nickname Silent Bob.*

Synonyms: laconic; reticent

Tawdry
adj
(<u>taw</u> dree)

· ·

Vicissitude
noun
(vih <u>sih</u> sih tood)

· ·

Vim
noun
(vihm)

gaudy; cheap; showy

> *The performer changed into her **tawdry**, spangled costume and stepped out onto the stage to do her show.*

Synonyms: flashy; loud; meretricious

. . . .

a change or variation; ups and downs

> *Investors must be prepared for **vicissitudes** of the stock market.*

Synonyms: inconstancy; mutability

. . . .

vitality and energy

> *The **vim** with which she worked so early in the day explained why she was so productive.*

Synonyms: force; power

Vituperate
verb
(vih <u>too</u> puhr ayt)

. . . .

Voluble
adj
(<u>vahl</u> yuh buhl)

. . . .

Zephyr
noun
(<u>zeh</u> fuhr)

to abuse verbally; berate

> *Vituperating someone is never a constructive way to effect change.*

Synonyms: castigate; reproach; scold

· ·

talkative; speaking easily; glib

> *The **voluble** man and his reserved wife proved the old saying that opposites attract.*

Synonyms: loquacious; verbose

· ·

a gentle breeze; something airy or unsubstantial

> *The **zephyr** from the ocean made the intense heat on the beach bearable for the sunbathers.*

Synonyms: breath; draft